"C. G. Jung characterized his psychology as an attempt, 'ever renewed, to give an answer to the question of the interplay between "here" and "hereafter".' Inspired by her own bereavement, Susan Olson soulfully engages the same interplay. Grappling now with the starkness of loss, now with the richness of death, she gives her answer to the 'here' and 'hereafter' question. A book of love and mystery. Highly recommended!"

Greg Mogenson, Jungian analyst, author of *Greeting the Angels: An Imaginal View of the Mourning Process*

"A truly psychological work. Grounded in personal experiences, and armed with wide-ranging knowledge and sensitivity, the author explores grief, transformation, and dreams of the dead in human psychology. This remarkable book can help us, professionally and personally, face the loss of a loved one and the legacy of the dead."

Paul Kugler, Jungian analyst, author of *Raids on the Unthinkable: Freudian and Jungian Psychoanalysis*

"Susan Olson follows the unconscious currents that shape and channel mourning. Her book is a generous, deeply moving, and personal gift to all whose hearts will never be unbroken after the loss of a child. Hearts may mend through a journey in the symbolic landscapes of dreams, where the beloved one lives on in a form scarcely recognized by our limited consciousness."

Kathrin Asper, Jungian analyst, author of *The Inner Child in Dreams*

I0095468

Images of the Dead in Grief Dreams

While in training at the C. G. Jung Institute in Zürich in 1988, Susan Olson suffered the loss of her daughter in an auto accident. In this intimate and unique exploration, Olson uses C. G. Jung's psychological framework to describe her journey through tragedy, guided by a series of vivid dreams.

In *Images of the Dead in Grief Dreams: A Jungian View of Mourning*, Jung's definition of the dream as a "harbinger of fate, a portent and comforter, a messenger of the gods" evolves from theory into embodied insight as Olson describes her encounter with the transforming power of grief. Drawing from personal experience as well as theoretical and clinical material, Olson presents premonitory dreams, which occur before the loss of a loved one, and grief dreams, which follow a loved one's death, and analyzes both according to Jung's method of dream interpretation. Sharing her own dreams as well as those of other mourners, Olson asserts that such dreams play a crucial role in the dreamer's emotional recovery and psychological development, otherwise known as the process of individuation. She sensitively offers an assessment of the stages of grief and draws on the Greek myth of Demeter and Persephone, Jung's memoirs, and other literature to amplify her experience of mourning. In this rare combination of grief theory and dream work, *Images of the Dead in Grief Dreams* is both a grief memoir and an extensive study of C. G. Jung's view of the mourning process.

This fully updated revised edition will be of immense interest to Jungian analysts and trainees, academics, psychologists, students of Jungian dream analysis, and to all who have suffered loss.

Susan Olson, M.A., L.C.S.W., graduated from the C. G. Jung Institute in Zürich, Switzerland, and is now a Jungian analyst in Atlanta, Georgia, U.S. She is on the faculty of the Memphis-Atlanta Jungian Seminar, an affiliate of the Inter-Regional Society of Jungian Analysts.

Images of the Dead in Grief Dreams

A Jungian View of Mourning

Susan Olson

Second Edition

Routledge
Taylor & Francis Group

LONDON AND NEW YORK

by Routledge
2 Park Square, Milton Park, Abingdon, Oxon OX14 4RN

and by Routledge
52 Vanderbilt Avenue, New York, NY 10017

Routledge is an imprint of the Taylor & Francis Group, an informa business

© 2021 Susan Olson

First edition published by Spring Journal Books, 2010

Second edition published 2021

British Library Cataloguing-in-Publication Data
A catalogue record for this book is available from the British Library

Library of Congress Cataloging-in-Publication Data
Names: Olson, Susan (Jungian analyst), author.
Title: Images of the dead in grief dreams : a jungian
view of mourning / Susan Olson.
Description: Second edition. | Abingdon, Oxon ; New York, NY : Routledge, 2021. |
First edition published by Spring Journal Books, 2010. |
Includes bibliographical references and index.
Identifiers: LCCN 2020009543 (print) | LCCN 2020009544 (ebook) |
ISBN 9780367441029 (hbk) | ISBN 9780367441036 (pbk) |
ISBN 9781003007630 (ebk)
Subjects: LCSH: Death–Psychological aspects. | Grief. | Dreams.
Classification: LCC BF789.D4 O39 2021 (print) |
LCC BF789.D4 (ebook) | DDC 155.9/37–dc23
LC record available at https://lccn.loc.gov/2020009543
LC ebook record available at https://lccn.loc.gov/2020009544

ISBN: 978-0-367-44102-9 (hbk)
ISBN: 978-0-367-44103-6 (pbk)
ISBN: 978-1-003-00763-0 (ebk)

Typeset in Times
by Newgen Publishing UK

In loving memory of Elizabeth
and with gratitude for my family

Contents

Preface

This book is a revised edition of my earlier work, *By Grief Transformed: Dreams and the Mourning Process,* published by Spring Journal Books in 2010. I am grateful to Routledge for providing the opportunity to republish my work and to Susannah Frearson, Heather Evans, Victoria Chow, Céline Durassier, and other members of the editorial staff for their prompt and careful editorial assistance as I revised the text.

The heart of both books is a series of vivid dreams that came to me in the two years following the death of my daughter Elizabeth in an auto accident in 1988. In those dreams, which led me through a long period of mourning, her image functioned as a companion in grief, a provider of gifts, a bearer of enigmatic messages, and a spiritual guide. My training as a Jungian analyst prompted me to study my dreams in depth and eventually to explore the role of dreams in the mourning process. I found ample supportive material in Jung's writings and in the work of other Jungian writers who have been touched by grief. As time went by, I also began to gather dreams from friends, colleagues, and workshop participants. When it came time to write about my experience, my intention was to present my own story as one of many: unique and yet remarkably similar to the stories of others who have suffered the loss of a loved one. I hoped to demonstrate that images of the dead in grief dreams play a crucial part in the archetypal experience of mourning.

To that end, in my first book I amplified my own and others' dream material with extensive allusions to mythology, literature, religious rituals, and cultural traditions. In this book I have omitted some of those amplifications and simplified others. I have eliminated some illustrations, but have added new written material when appropriate. The structure of this book is similar to that of the first one, except that one long chapter has been divided into two, one focusing on dream reunions in general and one devoted to Jung's dreams of his dead father. I have rewritten the entire text and hope that the result is a more focused, graceful, and concise book.

I would like to thank my family, friends, and colleagues for their enduring support as I have tackled this project for the second time. I am especially grateful to Mary Burke, Nancy Carter, Deborah Egger, Chris Slay, and Jacqueline Wright, who have given me permission to use their material in these pages. Elizabeth's friend Laura, who survived the accident, and Michael's mother Rita are always in my heart. Lee Lawson, whose painting of Demeter and Persephone graced the cover of my first book, has generously allowed me to use her new painting, also entitled "Demeter and Persephone," on the cover of the paperback edition of this one. Above all, my heartfelt gratitude goes to my son Rob and his wife Linda, my granddaughters Caroline and Becca, and my husband Don for their sustaining and loving presence.

Chapter 1

The open door

In an address given at the founding of the C. G. Jung Institute (Zürich) in 1948, Jung invited his students and colleagues to continue his study of "pre-catastrophal dreams, i.e., dreams occurring before accidents, illness, and death... The investigation of pre- and post-mortal psychic phenomena also comes into this category," he stated. "These are particularly important because of the relativization of space and time that accompanies them."[1] Many years later, pondering the meaning of a post-mortal dream of his wife, he wrote, "it is all-important for a disciplined imagination to build up images of intangibles by logical principles and on the basis of empirical data, that is, on the evidence of dreams."[2] The subjects of pre- and post-mortal dreams, the relativization of space and time, and the mystery of life after death fascinated Jung throughout his life. He never stopped wondering and speculating about them, and his close relationship with the unconscious provided him with abundant empirical data to stimulate his own "disciplined imagination."

I began analytic training in Zürich in 1987, almost forty years after the establishment of the Jung Institute. I had read *Memories, Dreams, Reflections* and some of Jung's other works, and I had experienced two post-mortal dreams myself, but I had never had a pre-catastrophal dream in my life. Then in early 1988, while I was at home on a long holiday break, I had an archetypal dream suggesting that my eighteen-year-old daughter Elizabeth, a first-year college student, might be in danger. The dream troubled me, but I did not know what to make of it and did not tell her about it. I recorded it in my dream journal, thinking that I would discuss it with my analyst later. Then I turned my attention to the activities of that busy time and almost forgot the dream altogether.

Back in Zürich, I came home one day to find in my mailbox a card announcing the opening of an exhibit featuring the work of an artist named Josef Polacek. The ethereal image on the card pictured a white arched doorway with white shuttered doors opening into a clear blue sky. A white heart was carved on the lintel, a few white clouds drifted through the open door, and sheer white curtains floated in the breeze. The only dark feature was a shadowy figure standing just behind the left-hand door.[3] I was drawn to the image and thought that Elizabeth would like it too, so I scribbled a quick note on the back of the card and mailed it to her. Then I forgot about it, just as I had forgotten my troubling dream two months earlier.

Five days later I was having dinner with my friend Terry in my tiny one-room apartment when the telephone rang. It was my son Rob, also a college student, calling from the U.S. I had talked to him earlier in the day and was surprised to hear from him again. But this time his voice sounded tense and strained. "Mom, I have terrible news," he said. "I don't know how to tell you this, so I'll just tell you. Elizabeth and Michael were killed last night in a hit-and-run auto accident in Canada. Laura was with them but she was not hurt. The guy who hit them turned himself in later. The police think that he was drunk."

My memories of the rest of that night are a blur. Terry offered to stay with me and I called two other friends, Diane and Nancy, who arrived within the hour. I remember making a reservation to fly home the next day, talking to Rob again and imploring him not to travel alone, throwing some clothes into a suit-case, spending a restless night with little sleep, and being told at the airport that I would have to furnish a copy of my daughter's death certificate to qualify for a reduced "death case" plane fare. On the plane I could not figure out how to turn off the airflow valve that was blowing cold air into my face. As the flight attendant explained the simple procedure (which I had done many times before), it occurred to me that I might be in shock. I don't remember crying. I could not eat, but I took the sleeping pill that one of my friends, a nurse, had given me. The plane was relatively empty and I was able to stretch out and rest fitfully for a few hours. But before I did, I looked through my dream journal and discovered the pre-catastrophal dream that I had almost forgotten. I was stunned. Had my uncon-scious tried to warn me of Elizabeth's death two months before it occurred? I was in no shape to address that question then, but I knew that one day I would have to look more closely into my dark, perplexing dream.

Certain images of the next few days are embedded in my memory. Rob and Elizabeth's stepfather, John, met me at the airport and drove home while Rob and I sat in the back seat, holding onto each other for dear life. The next day, as our family planned Elizabeth's service, we remembered that after her grandfather's recent funeral she had stated her wishes about what to do "if anything ever happened" to her. She would want her body to be cremated, she said, but she was adamant that there be no "fake grass" covering the ground when her ashes were buried. When we visited the cemetery, we picked out a plot in a remote corner that we thought she would have liked. In my imagination I could almost hear her saying, "Okay, mom, this one will do." Later at the funeral home we viewed her body, cold and bruised and wrapped in her grandfather's warm plaid bathrobe because her clothes were still in her college dorm room, hundreds of miles away. In a moment of inspiration, Rob asked the funeral director to snip off three locks of her long blonde hair—one for himself, one for her father, and one for me. Just before leaving the room I took one last look at her body and discovered that the ring she had always worn, in the shape of a small silver snake, was still coiled around the little finger of her right hand. It had accompanied her body through death and on the long plane ride home to Georgia. I was not afraid to touch her, but I was irrationally afraid that I would damage her hand if I tried to remove the ring. So the funeral director came to our aid again and did it for me. To this day, that little ring is one of my most cherished possessions.

In the days before and after the funeral, friends appeared at the door and provided more food and drink than we could possibly consume. Flowers and mail poured in. Elizabeth's roommate Laura, who had survived the accident, insisted on attending their friend Michael's funeral and then came to Elizabeth's as well. From her I learned that Elizabeth had never received the card that I had sent her. Laura had found it in their mailbox after the accident and now returned it to me. When I saw it again, I was as stunned as I had been when I discovered my dream on the plane home from Zürich. The image of the white door opening into the blue sky was a clear example of synchronicity, which Jung defined as a phenomenon in which premonitions or visions often correspond to an event in the outer world.[4] The card's arrival just before Elizabeth passed through the open door into eternity convinced me that synchronicity is not only a theory, but a very real experience.

At the cemetery we followed Elizabeth's wishes as best we could. Her ashes were placed in a beautiful but simple wooden box and buried deep in the Georgia red clay. No Astroturf covered the pile of earth nearby. We laid flowers in her grave and took turns shoveling dirt into the hole. Then we scattered more flowers on the bare ground. I was deeply moved but still unable to cry. I knew that I was encased in the shell of numbness that follows the death of a loved one and protects the psyche against unbearable pain. The numbness lasts until the psyche is able to withstand the waves of emotion that are about to break.

In early spring, the grass was still dry and brown in Georgia but daffodils and narcissus were beginning to poke their slender green stalks through the earth. On my visits to the cemetery I was touched to see the rocks, shells, and flowers that unknown visitors had left at Elizabeth's grave. Every day I arranged and rearranged the flowers that had arrived at my house, culling out the dead blossoms and preserving the living ones as long as I could. At last, when all had wilted and died, I gathered them up into one big bouquet and drove to the cemetery. I parked my car at the gravesite and walked down to the old bridge nearby. In a ritual of farewell, I dropped the dead flowers into the brown water and watched them disappear around the long lazy curve of the river. I stood there for a long time. At last I walked back to my car and drove home.

I knew that my tears were welling up inside, but still they would not flow. Then one night, about two weeks after her death, Elizabeth visited me in a dream, embraced me, and left me with an enigmatic message. She seemed as warm and vital and loving as ever. I felt as though she had been with me as a living presence. When I woke up and realized again that she had died, the floodgates opened and I was finally able to weep. But the cognitive dissonance was unnerving. How could she seem so alive when I knew very well that she was dead?

The synchronicities and dreams that I experienced during this time hint at the possibility of a transcendent level of reality existing beyond waking consciousness. As we struggle to describe it, images of place such as the spirit-world, the land of the dead, the underworld, the other side, and the kingdom of heaven come to mind, as do images of time such as the beyond, the eternal, and the hereafter. (It seems that we cannot help thinking in terms of time and space, even when we are trying to describe another level of reality.) However we imagine it, the other world remains hidden behind the open door, like the shadowy figure on the card I had sent to Elizabeth. Hints of it come in the form of premonitions and dreams which grip our emotions, challenge our thinking, and stretch our imaginations. They emanate from an intangible level of being that is just as "real" as the mundane world of time and space. We cannot see it with the naked eye or hear it with the naked ear, but the eyes and ears of the psyche can see and hear it, if we will open them, watch, and listen.

Several months after Elizabeth's death I went back to Zürich to resume my training. I knew that she would want me to continue and that I needed to be in analysis at that painful time. As I worked with two gifted analysts, I began to see that distinct themes and patterns were emerging in my dreams. In fact, my first postmortal dream was the beginning of a long dream series which continued for two more years. Elizabeth appeared in these dreams as a vivid presence, sometimes consoling me and sometimes needing consolation herself. Sometimes she spoke, but often she remained silent. She appeared in different clothes and experimented with new hairstyles, as if looking for just the right outfit to wear in the afterlife. She presented me with gifts and spoke cryptic words about the nature of the other world. Many of these dreams were painful, but some were positive, even joyful. The images that appeared in them are as real to me now as my memories of Elizabeth's eighteen years of mortal life. The dream sequence shaped my experience of grief and provided clues about the transformative experience of mourning. To use Jung's words, they constituted the empirical data that helped my psyche build up images of the intangible mystery of life after death.

At one point during those years I tried to write a paper about my dreams, but it soon became clear that it was far too soon for me to be objective about this personal material. Instead I became interested in related topics such as the funeral rites of other cultures and religious beliefs about the relationship between the living and the dead. Studying these subjects enlarged my limited perspective and provided a collective context for my personal experience. Finally, many years after Elizabeth's death, I began to write and lecture about my dreams. I felt that they were not meant for me alone, but might offer comfort and meaning to others as well. Finally I published my book *By Grief Transformed: Dreams and the Mourning Process* (New Orleans, LA: Spring Journal Books, 2010). This present book constitutes an extensive revision of that material.

Public response to my first book convinced me that dreaming about the dead is not an unusual experience. Workshop participants were relieved to tell their own dreams of the dead without being considered "weird" or "crazy." Often they began by saying, "I've never told this to anyone before, but…" Their pain was eased when they were able to recount their dreams without fear of judgment or condemnation. Bereaved people have told me that my book has helped them understand their own grief dreams. That is gratifying to hear, because unfortunately the notion that dream images of the dead are pathological is still widespread today. The boundary between sanity and psychosis is precarious during the acute phase of grief. Visual and auditory hallucinations can be symptoms of a serious psychic disturbance, but it is possible to distinguish psychotic symptoms from dreams in which the dead appear to an otherwise intact person. Is the dreamer able to think symbolically, maintaining the distinction between imaginal and "actual" reality, or is he or she unable to tell the difference? Even in deep grief, an intact ego is able to maintain its objectivity, whereas in psychosis it shatters and identifies with powerful affects and images. For example, a dream in which a dead loved one appears and beckons to the dreamer can be interpreted symbolically, as a summons to explore the deeper meaning of the experience of loss, or literally, as an invitation to suicide. The ability to distinguish between the two is essential in determining what is pathological and what is not.

In his 1902 doctoral dissertation, "On the Psychology and Pathology of So-Called Occult Phenomena," Jung studied the dreams and visions of his young cousin Helene Preiswerk.[5] There he concluded that "psychic powers emerge from psychological states of mind and have nothing to do with the so-called supernatural."[6] But as Paul Kugler notes, later in life Jung began to regard dreams of the dead as psychic facts and to regard them with curiosity and an open mind.[7] From this perspective Jung approached dream images of the dead on several levels: interpreted subjectively, they may represent aspects of the dreamer's own psyche; viewed objectively, they can be regarded as spirits of the departed; from an imaginal perspective, they invite us to explore the mysteries of the objective psyche. When taken together, these three approaches lead to a deeper understanding of ourselves, the realm of the unconscious, and perhaps the world of the dead as well.

In *Memories*, written near the end of his life, Jung devotes an entire chapter to the subject of life after death. There he states that dreams help us form a view of immortality by providing hints from the unconscious. Usually we dismiss these hints because we think that "the question is not susceptible to answer." He goes on to suggest that we abandon the question as an intellectual problem and "build up a conception on the basis of such hints," even though it will remain a hypothesis which can never be proved.[8] In other words, dreams can help us build up our own notion of what happens to our loved ones (and to ourselves) after death. Do the dead survive in some form? Are they transformed into pure spirit, or do they vanish into thin air? Do they know that they have died? Can they still communicate with us? Can *we* communicate with *them*? Do they grieve as we do? Does the process of individuation continue after death? These questions cannot be answered on an intellectual level, but dreams provide the raw material we need to formulate our own tentative answers.

Bereavement dreams serve as a guide on the precarious path of grief. They track the process of mourning, showing us where we are on the map and providing clues about where we are going. Dream images of the dead can provide unexpected comfort and counsel, as though the dead are teaching us how to allow grief to inform and transform our souls. As Greg Mogenson observes, "[t]he way the dead appear to us in our dreams and fantasies, the things they say and do, present the logos of the psyche, the logic and culture of the mind... Mourning, we must never forget, is an intensely creative process."[9]

Mourning is an archetypal experience, common to all human beings and organized around universal themes and images. My own grief journey was inseparable from the dreams that animated and informed it. But my own story is just one of many. Therefore this book includes many of Jung's dreams, as reported in *Memories*, as well as dreams told by others and examples from mythology, religion, and literature. By including this material I hope to amplify my singular experience, explore the archetypal dimension of grief, and examine the power of mourning to catalyze emotional, psychological, and spiritual transformation.

In his remarks at the founding of the Institute, Jung mentioned two types of pre- and post-mortal psychic phenomena: dreams that occur before accidents, illness, and death, and dreams that follow the death of a loved one. The next two chapters of this book explore the subject of pre-catastrophal dreams, beginning with my own dream and then turning to dreams related by Jung and others. Later chapters present bereavement dreams from each of the so-called "stages of grief." Exploring this material has often reminded me of the familiar words of the poet Rainer Maria Rilke, in which he encourages a young poet to be patient with what is unsolved in his heart and learn to love the questions themselves. If we live the questions, writes Rilke, one day we may discover that we have lived right into the answers.[10] I encourage the reader to approach this book with an open mind, a receptive heart, and a curious spirit. May you cherish and live into your questions, be wary of easy answers, and allow your disciplined imagination to build up images and concepts based on the empirical evidence of your own dreams as well as the dreams recounted here.

Notes

1   C. G. Jung, *The Symbolic Life*, *CW* 18, § 1138. All further references to Jung's *Collected Works* (hereafter abbreviated *CW*) are from the Routledge edition.
2   C. G. Jung, *Memories, Dreams, Reflections*, 341. Hereafter referred to in the text and notes as *Memories*.
3   Unfortunately I did not write down the title of this painting or attend the exhibit. I have tried without success to locate Josef Polacek, but I have found him to be as elusive as the shadowy figure behind the open door.
4   Cf. C. G. Jung, *Memories*, 258.
5   C. G. Jung, "On the Psychology and Pathology of Occult Phenomena," *Psychiatric Studies*, *CW* 1, § 1–150.

6 D. Bair, *Jung: A Biography*, 63.

7 P. Kugler, *Raids on the Unthinkable*, 113ff.

8 C. G. Jung, *Memories*, 332.

9 G. Mogenson, *Greeting the Angels*, xi–xii.

10 The last two sentences paraphrase a quote found in Rainer Maria Rilke's *Letters to a Young Poet*, 21.

Chapter 2

Running with the horses

Precognitive dreams

The word "precognitive," derived from two Latin roots meaning "before" and "know," refers to "foreknowledge of an event, especially foreknowledge of a paranormal kind." Similarly, the word "premonitory" is derived from Latin roots meaning "before" and "warn."[1] Thus precognitive and premonitory dreams foretell or forewarn the dreamer of impending events, often involving accidents, illness, or death. But where do these dreams originate? As Jung observes, we cannot ascribe them to our own powers, because we do not know until sometime later that they represent "foreknowledge, or knowledge of something that happened at a distance."[2] Precognitions and premonitions do not derive from the conscious ego, but emerge from a level of the unconscious that seems to exist beyond time and space. Jung had many precognitive dreams in his life and considered them legitimate contents of the unconscious, although he could do no more than speculate about how the unconscious knows things of which the ego is unaware.

A nightmare

Precognitive and premonitory dreams often take the form of vivid nightmares which leave the dreamer emotionally shaken, speechless, and gasping for breath. In fact the word "nightmare" is derived from a medieval superstition that female spirits called "mares... might behave like succubae, settling on top of the bodies of sleeping men, choking off their breath, and taking away their power of speech, hence the [term] nightmare."[3] Two months before Elizabeth's death I had this dream, which began peacefully but soon became a nightmare:

> Elizabeth and I are at the beach. We swim for a while and then get out of the water and lie on the dock. When we look out to sea we notice that the tide is going out, exposing large stretches of sand which had been under water. The atmosphere becomes charged and heavy, as it does just before a storm. The whole landscape is bathed in eerie red light.

Then we see a herd of horses out in the water, running back and forth from one sandbar to another. They run from left to right and back again as if choreographed, their manes and tails streaming out behind them. We look at them closely and see that they are no ordinary horses. They are running on their hind legs and seem to be people wearing horse costumes, with their human feet sticking out below. Each time they reach a certain point on the left, a few of them vanish into thin air. Then the rest of the herd turns around and runs back to the right again.

I feel cautious and do not want to get too close to these strange creatures. But Elizabeth is curious and wades into the water to investigate. As I watch, she begins to run with the horses, from left to right and back again. Then all of a sudden she turns into a horse herself. I am very frightened and wade out to see what has happened. But before I can reach her, she and all the horses disappear. I run to the place where I last saw her. On the sand is a small suitcase with a few things in it—a doll, a coat, and some other small objects. I also see a small spot of blood on the sand at the spot where she disappeared. I wake up terrified, calling her name.

This is the dream that I forgot, then rediscovered in my journal on the plane trip home the day after Elizabeth's death. It had occurred two months earlier at the end of a long Christmas holiday, just before she went back to college and I returned to Zürich to resume my training. At the time I thought that the dream might reflect my anxiety about our impending separation, but its tone suggested something more ominous. I did not tell her the dream, but of course I wondered later what might have happened if I had. Could her fatal accident have been averted? Are there such things as accidents, or are certain events meant to happen? Can we alter the course of the future, or are we powerless to change it? Such questions are not unusual in the aftermath of a disaster, but as Jung observed, they are "not susceptible to answer."

Jung's approach to dreams

The Jungian interpretation of dreams, often referred to as *amplification*, involves noting the dreamer's personal associations to dream images, with special attention paid to the initial setting, characters, action, and resolution. After personal associations have been gathered, the dreamer and analyst take note of any archetypal images and symbols that may be present. The term "archetype," in Jungian thought, refers to universal patterns of instinct and behavior found in all ethnic, religious, and cultural traditions. Jung defines the archetype as an "unconscious, pre-existent form that [is] part of the inherited structure of the psyche and can… manifest itself spontaneously anywhere, at any time."[4] We cannot apprehend archetypes directly, but we can observe their presence in myths, literature, folklore, religious rituals, art, and dreams. Dream images such as the beach, the sea, and the horses, drawn from everyday life, often have archetypal significance as well.

The setting of a dream provides essential clues to its meaning. My personal association to the beach setting of my dream reminds me of lazy summer vacations spent splashing in the waves and strolling along the shore hunting for shells. As the dream opens, Elizabeth and I enjoy this relaxed, carefree atmosphere, swimming for a while and then lying on the dock in the sunshine.[5] But before long the sun disappears behind the clouds and the atmosphere darkens, as though a storm is brewing. In actual life, this would be the time to fold up the beach chairs, gather the towels, and head for the nearest shelter. But this is not what happens in the dream. Instead, Elizabeth and I remain on the beach and watch as the ebbing tide exposes previously submerged sandbars to the eerie red light. Before our eyes, the sunny beach transforms into a shadowy, ominous landscape.

Shifting to the archetypal level of interpretation, if dry land is an image of the *terra firma* of waking consciousness, then the sea represents the unfathomable depths of the unconscious, "the maternal womb of all psychic being."[6] Thus the beach, with its ebbing and flowing tides, is a symbol of the ever-changing fluid boundary between the two. When the tide goes out in the dream, the sea-bed of the unconscious, usually submerged beneath the waves, is revealed to the light. In psychological terms, a lowering of the level of consciousness is occurring and the focus of attention is moving to a deeper level of the psyche that is usually hidden from view. In this precarious place the ego, the organ of psychic consciousness, is no longer in charge, and forces beyond human control soon enter the scene.

Many years after this dream, I read a thesis by Jungian analyst Jerry Wright entitled "Archetypal *Thin Places*," in which he notes that Celtic mythology contains abundant images of watery thin places such as rivers, lakes, wells, and the sea. In these places the veil between this world and the next was thought to be so porous that "spirits and mortals [could] pass [through] with relative ease."[7] Furthermore, "[i]n Irish mythology there are many stories of heroes and other individuals crossing through the watery *thin places*, either by accident or having been led there by magic animals."[8] The beach in my dream can be interpreted as such an archetypal thin place, with the strange horses representing the magic animals of Irish myth. In addition to thin places, there are thin times such as birthdays, holidays, and the moment of death, during which the veil between the two worlds is especially permeable. My dream came as Elizabeth and I were approaching such a thin place and time, although we were not aware of it then. By portraying her death as an instance of an individual being led through a watery thin place by magic animals, the dream points beyond personal experience to the archetypal level of meaning.

The next step in Jungian dream interpretation involves taking note of the characters in the dream and their relationship to the dreamer. Jung suggests two possible approaches to interpreting dream characters. If the figure in question is known to the dreamer, it may be interpreted either *subjectively*, as an aspect of the dreamer's own psyche, or *objectively*, as an image of an actual person in the outer world. Thus the dream figure of Elizabeth, interpreted subjectively, might represent an unconscious shadow aspect of my personality. (Jung used the term "shadow" to refer to attitudes, values, and character traits unknown or unacceptable to ego-consciousness.) Interpreting her image objectively would refer to her as an objective, existing being. (Remember that she was still alive at the time of this dream.) Either way, the dream suggests that the dream-ego (the "I" in the dream) adopts a cautious "wait and see" attitude to the horses, while Elizabeth seems fearless and wades right out to meet them, unaware of her own danger. In fact, I learned later that she and her friends had not been careful enough on the night of the accident, when their car ran out of gas and they walked along the side of a dimly lit highway to get help, wearing dark clothing that could not be seen by passing drivers. But whether one interprets the two dream figures subjectively or objectively, their contrasting attitudes are quite apparent. This contrast reminded me of two "real life" events that had occurred on a mountain vacation when Elizabeth was about thirteen. Near our rental cottage was an overgrown field in which we often saw four or five small brown horses grazing. Elizabeth, who had some riding experience, would climb over the fence to offer them an apple or a piece of carrot, while I watched carefully from a distance. On the same vacation we drove to a small mountain lake to swim. Elizabeth plunged right into the cold water and urged me to join her, but I preferred to wade in step by step and get used to the temperature gradually. The setting of my dream was not identical to this vacation spot, but the images of the horses and the water were familiar, and our respective attitudes corresponded exactly to our "real life" positions.

The dream image of the mysterious horses invites further archetypal amplification. Jung noted the link between nightmare and "mare" when he observed that some Germanic words for *mare* are similar to the Old English and Norse *mara*, meaning "ogress, incubus, [or] demon."[9] The archetypal image of the horse, he wrote, "has to do with sorcery and magical spells—especially the black night-horses which herald death."[10] The horses in my dream appear as the dream is changing from an "ordinary" dream into a nightmare. As they mysteriously disappear into thin air and lead Elizabeth with them, they certainly seem to be magical animals and heralds of death.

A further amplification of the horse image can be found in Marie-Louise von Franz's book *On Dreams and Death,* in which she discusses the premonitory dream of a cavalry officer four weeks before his unexpected death. In his dream, the decomposed carcass of a horse lying in a lead coffin foreshadows the death of his animal body, the "instinctive part of his physical nature which 'carries' him." Von Franz interprets the dream as a shock "meant to detach the dreamer from his body" and to prepare him for his imminent death.[11] She compares the dead horse in the coffin to the body of Osiris in his coffin in Egyptian mythology.

In fact, horses are associated with death in many religious and mythological traditions. In Germanic mythology the steeds of Wotan's " 'wild hunt,' made up of the souls of the dead," were often pictured as gray cloud-horses with "their feet on backward."[12] The Valkyries, winged daughters of Wotan, could become horses themselves or "come on their cloud-horses and carry dead warriors to Valhalla."[13] Celtic mythology refers to a magic spirit-animal called a "Pooka," which could take either human or horse form and was regarded as an omen of death. It could also appear as a Kelpie, a water spirit in the form or a "white horse whose mane was like the foaming crests of the waves."[14] In ancient Greek literature, the horse Xanthus in Homer's *Iliad* is associated with death because he weeps for Patroclus and later warns Achilles of his approaching death. In Greek mythology Hades, the god of death, "[o]n the rare occasions when he left his gloomy underworld and visited the surface of the earth," drove a chariot drawn by four coal-black horses.[15] On one of those occasions he abducted the goddess Persephone and carried her off into his underground kingdom—a tale to which I shall return in Chapter 4.

In summary, I understand the horses in my dream as archetypal harbingers of death shrouded in skins which both conceal and reveal their true nature. They appear and vanish instantaneously, indicating that they can travel easily between worlds. In the major action of the dream, Elizabeth joins them, is transformed into one of them and vanishes into thin air. Like Persephone being carried off into the underworld, she disappears suddenly and with no warning. And once she is gone, I cannot get her back. The remainder of the dream's action is almost an anti-climax, as I run into the water to retrieve the objects she has left behind. The resolution of the dream comes as I wake up, realize she is gone, and call out her name.

Transitional objects

The last time I saw Elizabeth alive she was boarding a plane, her shoulders draped with bags full of clothes, books, and snacks—all the gear needed by a first-year college student returning to school. In her characteristic fashion, she gave me a kiss and a hug, turned, and walked through the door to the gangway without looking back. (This was before 9/11, when it was still possible to accompany a departing passenger all the way to the gate.) Several days later I boarded a plane myself, similarly laden with my own baggage. On our outer journeys, we needed all the paraphernalia jammed into our carry-on bags. But on her final journey, Elizabeth needed nothing at all, not even the small suitcase lying on the sand at the end of my dream.

Thanks to the British child psychiatrist D. W. Winnicott, I think of the suitcase now as a "transitional object," a term he coined refer to an infant's first " 'not-me' possession." For example, Elizabeth had a baby blanket which became her transitional object during her first few years of life. To use Winnicott's language, she "found" it in her crib as an infant but she also "created" it by becoming attached to it, investing it with meaning, and using it as "a defence against anxiety, especially anxiety of depressive type."[16] It helped her calm down when she was upset, go to sleep when she was restless, and feel safe in new or frightening surroundings. In Winnicott's words, it became "absolutely necessary at bed-time or at time[s] of loneliness or when a depressed mood threaten[ed]."[17] As she grew older, she used it to swaddle the dolls and stuffed animals that gradually took its place. After countless launderings, it finally fell to pieces and her attachment to it diminished. But a small fragment survived and now serves as a transitional object linking me to her. Transitional objects occupy the symbolic area which Winnicott dubbed the realm of "illusion," the "transitional space" between the inner and outer world. In this "intermediate area between the subject and that which is object-ively perceived," the transitional object becomes the child's first symbol.[18] When a child's mother is absent it links the child to her, and it is also the child's first cre-ation. True transitional objects, writes Winnicott, become "more important than the mother, an almost inseparable part of the infant."[19] No longer mere blankets or toys, they are suffused with symbolic meaning.

As a transitional object, the suitcase in my dream represents the holding cap-acity of what Jung called the "Self" with a capital "S," the central archetype of order that "embraces not only the conscious but also the unconscious psyche."[20] When trauma occurs, the Self contains the intense affects and images that threaten to overwhelm the embattled ego. Without this central organizing and containing principle, the psyche would shatter, leading to neurosis, dissociation, and even psychosis. When a loved one dies, her possessions become transitional objects that symbolize her continuing presence. Perhaps that is why the distribution of objects after death is so often fraught with emotion. Economic worth may not matter, even when things are financially valuable. Clothing, books, furniture, jew-elry, and art are no longer mere "things." They were worn, touched, or created by the dead loved one and still contain traces of her energy.

In her book *The Year of Magical Thinking*, written after her husband's sudden death, Joan Didion writes that she could not throw away his faded sweatshirt or give away his shoes because he might come back and need them again.[21] I remember the painful process of sorting through Elizabeth's clothes, books, and pictures, deciding what to keep, what to discard, and what to give away. A gum wrapper, a chewed pencil, even an old ratty sock became as precious as rare jewels. Thanks to her father I inherited her computer, which still had a drop of spilled coffee on its frame. It took me a long time to be able to wipe that spot away. Even now I wear some of her clothing, treasure things she made, and cherish gifts she gave me. When my granddaughters were little girls, I gave them many of her books, toys, and stuffed animals. Now they have inherited some of her clothing. Like the contents of the suitcase in my dream, Elizabeth's possessions still connect us to her more than thirty years after her death.

The little doll in the suitcase reminds me of the doll in the fairy tale "Wasilisa the Beautiful," a Russian variation of the Cinderella story. (I like this version because Elizabeth was studying Russian language and literature, and had traveled to Russia twice on school-sponsored trips.) As the tale opens, Wasilisa's dying mother gives her daughter a doll and instructs her to keep it with her always, feed it, and ask it for help if she loses her way. The girl puts the doll in her pocket and takes it with her on her visit to the Baba Yaga, the old witch in the woods. Obeying her mother's instructions, she feeds the doll and takes good care of it. In return, the doll guides Wasilisa on her journey, warns her of danger, and helps her complete the Baba Yaga's seemingly impossible tasks. Thus the dead mother, through the agency of the doll, helps her daughter grow into a mature young woman who is ready to make her way in the world. In my dream, the little doll in the suitcase reminded me that Elizabeth's creative, adventurous feminine spirit was still with me, even though she was not. In the ensuing years her spirit has guided and helped me face many difficult life challenges.

At the end of my dream, Elizabeth puts on a horse-skin and leaves her coat behind. She no longer needs the protection of the warm garment that shielded her from rain, snow, and stormy weather. Perhaps she leaves the coat knowing that I will need its literal and symbolic protection to face the seemingly impossible task of mourning for her. In the initial days of grief our bodies respond by going into shock. Our core temperature drops, we shiver with cold, and even indoors we may need to wear extra layers of clothing. We also need the protection of the psychological defenses that shield us from unbearable pain during the initial days of mourning. Eventually, as the so-called "stages of grief" unfold, we learn to put on and take off our literal and symbolic coats as needed. They provide security that we can choose to wear or not, depending upon our state of emotional vulnerability at the time.

The final image in the dream is the spot of blood on the sand, a symbol of the "blood ties" between relatives. According to Barbara Walker, the Bible "views blood as the primary symbol of the life force…, because all the ancients were convinced that living people were literally made of their mothers' uterine blood, retained and coagulated into the form of a baby."[22] At the time of death, spilled blood represents the final outpouring of life energy. The spot of blood in my dream represents the last drop of Elizabeth's life force, but it also hints that although she is dead, our mother–daughter blood connection survives.

A painful blow of fate

At the time of my premonitory dream I was not familiar with the Celtic image of the thin place, the archetypal symbol of the horse, Winnicott's concept of transitional objects, or the tale of "Wasilisa the Beautiful." Nevertheless the unconscious "used" these images to forewarn me about the disaster that was about to occur and to give me exactly the images I would need as I mourned for Elizabeth. My terrifying dream of the horses certainly convinced me that precognitive experience is real, and opened my mind to the possibility that the "ordinary" world of space and time is only one aspect of a complex and mysterious universe.

In her previously cited book *Apparitions*, Aniela Jaffé suggests that premonitory dreams prepare us for an "imminent and painful blow of fate by experiencing it beforehand in the mind: it is a kind of rehearsal."[23] Such dreams also help us "establish a meaning in the sequence of events," she writes. "People are much more ready to submit to a fate that has a meaning than to one which is blind and inscrutable."[24] Elizabeth's death was a painful blow of fate that seemed altogether "blind and inscrutable" at the time. And yet my dream prepared me for it and became the prologue to a dream series that eventually helped me "establish a meaning in the sequence of events." But I must admit that in the days immediately following her death, the possibility of meaning seemed very remote indeed.

Notes

1 *New Oxford American Dictionary*, online edition.
2 C. G. Jung, *Memories*, 373.
3 B. Walker, *The Woman's Dictionary of Symbols and Sacred Objects*, 75.
4 C. G. Jung, *Memories*, 411.
5 When writing about the dream figures of Elizabeth and others, I am referring to their dream images and not to the persons themselves.
6 Aniela Jaffé, *Apparitions*, 32.
7 Jerry R. Wright, "Archetypal *Thin Places*: Experiencing the Numinosum," 17.
8 *Ibid.*, 9.
9 C. G. Jung, *CW 5*, § 370.
10 *Ibid.*, § 371–373.
11 Both quotes are from M.-L. von Franz, *On Dreams and Death*, 19.
12 B. Walker, *The Woman's Dictionary*, 379.
13 *Ibid.*
14 *Ibid.*
15 B. Hannah, *The Cat, Dog, and Horse Lectures*, 111.
16 D. W. Winnicott, *Playing and Reality*, 4.
17 *Ibid.*
18 *Ibid.*, 3.
19 *Ibid.*, 7.
20 C. G. Jung, *Memories*, 417.
21 J. Didion, *The Year of Magical Thinking*, 37.
22 B. Walker, *The Woman's Dictionary*, 299.
23 A. Jaffé, *Apparitions*, 20.
24 *Ibid.*, 19.

Chapter 3

Incomprehensible things

Jung's premonitory dreams

Throughout his life Jung experienced potent visions, dreams, premonitions, and other "paranormal" events. After years of study he came to regard such experiences as hints from the unconscious about "things which by all logic we could not possibly know."[1] In an anthology of interviews entitled *C. G. Jung Speaking*, he wrote that he had "analyzed forty-one dreams which forecast grave illness or death."[2] He also devoted an entire chapter of *Memories* to the subject of life after death, stating that his own dreams and those of others had helped him shape his views of the afterlife.[3] He concluded that although we cannot be certain about things which we do not understand rationally, nevertheless "it is important and salutary to speak also of incomprehensible things."[4]

Jung's accounts of his own premonitory dreams assume that the dreams refer to actual events and not to inner psychic processes. For example, he recounts a dream in which his wife's bed appeared as a grave-like pit with stone walls. While still asleep, he heard a deep sigh, as if someone were taking their last breath. Then he saw a female figure wearing a white gown sit up and float upwards. At that point he woke up, awakened his wife, noted the time of the dream, and thought at once that it might refer to a death.[5] The next morning he and his wife received the news that one of her cousins had died at the same time as his dream. In another dream Jung's sister, who had died several years earlier, appeared with a woman he knew well. In the dream he knew who the woman was, but upon waking he could not remember. Even so, he knew that she was going to die. His premonition was confirmed several weeks later when he heard that a former patient had died in an accident. At once he remembered her as the woman in his dream.[6] Although Jung considered the possibility that premonitory dreams such as these may have had a subjective meaning, he interpreted them objectively, as though they concerned the fate of the actual person. Of course, this view was validated by the later occurrence of an event or by the dreamer's discovery that an event had befallen at the same time as the dream.

People who have premonitory dreams often fear that they have *caused* an accident or death and believe that they might have been able to avert it. For example,

I often asked myself if I had been instrumental in the chain of events leading to Elizabeth's death, and I wondered if I could have done anything to prevent it. But Jung stresses that causality is not the operative principle in premonitory experiences. Citing J. B. Rhine's experiments on extrasensory perception, which had impressed him deeply, he writes that at times the psyche "functions outside of the spatio-temporal law of causality.... [W]e must face the fact that our world... relates to another order of things lying behind or beneath it." He concludes that he had become convinced that "part of our psychic existence is characterised by a relativity of space and time."[7]

In support of this view, Jung cites several examples of his own precognitive and after-death dreams involving a pupil, two friends, and a figure which he interprets as an ancestral spirit.[8] He also relates two premonitory dreams having to do with the unexpected death of his mother in 1923. The first dream occurred four months before her death and involved a conversation with his father, who had died in 1896. In the dream Jung's father wanted to consult his son on the subject of marital psychology. But before he could reply, Jung woke up wondering why his father should be seeking information on such problems. Only after his mother's death did he think that his dream might have been a premonition. Acknowledging that his parents did not have a happy relationship, Jung reasoned that perhaps his father, knowing that his wife would soon be joining him in the afterlife, needed some professional advice about a new approach to marriage.[9] Jung woke up before he could respond to his father, but as Greg Mogenson notes, he eventually "did answer the question his father had put to him. Following his mother's death he wrote 'Marriage as a Psychological Relationship' (1925)," in which he addressed the concerns his father had raised in the dream.[10]

The second dream occurred while Jung was on holiday, the night before he received the news of his mother's sudden death. In the dream he was in a gloomy forest in which huge boulders lay about among jungle-like trees. Suddenly he heard a piercing whistle and a huge wolfhound burst through the underbrush. The blood froze in his veins and he suddenly knew that "the Wild Huntsman had commanded it to carry away a human soul."[11] He awoke in terror, and the next day he heard of his mother's passing. In his comments on the dream, Jung does not consider a subjective interpretation. At first he thought that the Wild Huntsman was the devil, but later he concluded that the figure represented Wotan, the god of his German ancestors, who had carried his mother's soul into the "wholeness of nature and spirit in which conflicts and contradictions are resolved."[12] Nevertheless, his emotional conflict was intense. On the train home the next night, he thought he heard dance music and laughter, but another side of himself was full of terror and grief. Commenting on this experience years later, he observed that it presents death from two seemingly contradictory points of view. From the perspective of the ego, death is "a fearful piece of brutality" that "can so embitter us that we conclude there is no merciful God, no justice, and no kindness." But from the point of view of the Self, it is a joyful event in which the soul finally achieves wholeness.[13]

Jung's reflections on his dreams avoid exploration of personal issues such as his marital situation and his complicated relationship with his mother. Therefore he does not emphasize the subjective level of interpretation, but moves quickly to the objective level. While it would be fascinating to have Jung's perspective on his close relationships, "his distaste for exposing his personal life to the public eye was well known."[14] It may also be that as he neared the end of his life, personal history was of less importance to him than his emerging view of life after death. By interpreting his premonitory dreams as hints about the nature of the afterlife, he challenges us to examine our own experience and to form our own view of it.

Apparitions

Jung was certainly not alone in his fascination with the subject of life after death. In the mid-1950s the journal *Schweizerischer Beobachter* published a series of articles on prophetic dreams, premonitions, and visions. The editor asked readers to report such experiences and was astounded to receive more than 1,200 responses. He sent the material to Jung, who turned it over to his secretary Aniela Jaffé, an analyst and author in her own right. Her resulting book, *Apparitions: An Archetypal Approach to Death Dreams and Ghosts*, contains dreams and visions recounted by ordinary Swiss people. For example, a man who had been estranged from a friend reported this dream:

> I had quarreled with a friend and he had really hurt me. From then on I avoided him. Two years later I... dreamt that [he] had come and asked me to forgive him. When I turned a deaf ear to his plea, he came up to me and said: "For heaven's sake, don't be so obstinate! Something is awaiting me, that's why I want to be at peace." With these words he took hold of my hand—I felt a cold hand quite definitely. Then I awoke, only to find that the dream figure had vanished. But I heard the sound of a door shutting even though I was wide awake.[15]

Two days later the dreamer learned that his friend had died in an accident at the exact time of his dream. Distraught, he consulted a priest and asked if his unforgiving attitude might disturb the peace of his friend's soul. The priest advised him to forgive his friend, pay for a Mass to be said on his behalf, and attend the service in person. The dreamer did so and reported that he felt at peace and never had such dreams again.

Jaffé offers two possible interpretations of this dream: objectively, the figure of the friend may represent his "ghost" or spirit, but subjectively, it may be seen as an image of the dreamer's feeling function, which he split off when he quarreled with his friend. It may be that there is truth in both points of view. What matters in the end is that the dreamer reclaimed his feeling function, forgave his friend, and repaired the breach between them. According to Jaffé, the motif of forgiveness occurs often in premonitory dreams, especially if there is unfinished business between the dreamer and the deceased. Not surprisingly, another common motif is the theme of leave-taking. For instance, a woman dreamed that she met her brother-in-law, whom she had not seen for many years, on a path in the woods. "I called out a cheerful greeting to him," she wrote. He "smiled and waved back, but when we were about ten yards from each other, he turned down another path, smiled at me again and once more waved his hand." She was "quite taken aback" by this vivid dream and lay awake for hours thinking about it. The next day she received the news that her brother-in-law had died.[16]

It is one thing to read such accounts in a book, and quite another to hear them with one's own ears. Several years ago, a Jungian colleague and close friend of mine recounted a farewell dream involving her friend "Barbara," who had been battling cancer:

> I'm sweeping my house and Barbara is there, sitting on the bed. Then we're standing up facing each other and another woman is with us, embracing both of us. I don't remember our words, but it is clearly a farewell. The other woman says something to let us know it is time to say goodbye.

Although my friend was thousands of miles away from Barbara at the time, she felt strongly that they had said their final farewell. She noted the time of the dream, and the next morning she learned that Barbara had died at exactly that time. Later she learned that Barbara's daughter had also awakened at that moment, knowing that her mother was in trouble and feeling compelled to pray for her. My friend felt strongly that the dream figure of Barbara represented her actual friend, and not an aspect of her own psyche. She interpreted the other woman in the dream as a Great Mother figure who transcended the boundaries of time and space, embraced the two friends and helped them contain the sorrow of their parting. Jaffé asserts that dreams in which a mother figure performs a nurturing function indicate that the dreamer has a close relationship with the unconscious and a firm "rootedness in the instinctual life."[17] My friend's dream validates her own positive relationship with the unconscious as well as her close connection to her friend.

Images and symbols of death

Premonitory dreams often depict death in the form of vivid images and symbols. In her book *A Time to Mourn*, Verena Kast tells the story of a young woman named Elena whose boyfriend, George, had died suddenly of a heart attack. The night before his first attack Elena dreamed of an avalanche, but did not immediately relate the dream to George's illness. George also had several dreams which may have presaged his death, including images of runaway horses and a forest destroyed by a storm. While George was in the hospital on a heart monitor, Elena dreamed:

> I see a monitor screen. The upper half is bright, the lower half is darker. Three beams of light run across this screen, from right to left. After one beam of light crosses a third of the screen, it drops suddenly, as though extinguished. Then I realize that it is continuing its path down below in the darker half. I think of George and am frightened... I wake up and am deeply disturbed.[18]

After this dream Elena felt that George would not survive, and in fact he died the next day. But the image of the monitor screen suggested to her that his "light" had fallen into another sphere and was continuing on its way. Previously skeptical about life after death, she was now "convinced that someone whom one has loved cannot die, that he lives on in some form not recognized, or scarcely recognized, by our limited consciousness." Her dream brought comfort by giving her "the chance to develop a philosophy of life in which the dead, even if in a way not easily recognized, continue to be with us."[19]

Eighteen months before her sixteen-year-old son's death in a fight, Jungian analyst Geri Grubbs dreamed that intruders entered her apartment through a window. One of them struck her son on the head with a tennis racket and killed him. The next day (still in the dream) she cried hard and asked a "male presence" if this really had to happen. "Is he really dead?" she asked. "Yes, he's dead," the man replied. Then she was awakened by the primitive sound of a rattle, recorded her dream, and returned to "the twilight state." As she dozed, she felt the body of a "large, fat snake" wrapped around her neck. "The snake [felt] unusually warm and comforting for such an experience," she writes.[20] In analyzing her dream, which I have condensed here, Grubbs writes that "a sense of impending doom was constellated in my unconscious so strongly that I felt haunted with the sensations that [my son's] life would be a short one." Apparently he felt the same thing, for after his death she learned that he had told his friends a dream in which he died in a fight. On the day of his funeral she discovered a poem that he had written two months earlier, containing images of fighting, killing, slashing, and breaking bones. Grubbs identified the snake in her dream as "the animal of Aesculapius," the Greek god of healing, and concluded that her prophetic dream appeared to be "a preparation for what was to come. It seemed to be revealing that, even though I would suffer the catastrophic loss of my son, I would be cared for and healed by the archetypes of the soul."[21]

In 1944 Jung suffered a near-fatal heart attack. While he hovered between life and death, he had a near-death experience and a premonitory vision. He felt that he was floating high above the earth and could look down and see the globe "bathed in gloriously blue light." Then an image of his doctor in the "primal form" of the basileus (prince) of Kos floated up and silently told him that it was not yet time for him to leave this earth. When the vision ceased, Jung was dismayed to find himself once again in the three-dimensional world of time and space. He felt "violent resistance" to his physician and wrote that three weeks passed before he decided to live again. He saw great significance in his doctor's appearance in the archetypal form of the prince of Kos, because the Greek island of Kos was the site of the temple of Asclepius, the god of healing, and the birth-place of Hippocrates, the father of modern medicine. Jung interpreted his vision to mean that having assumed his "primal form," his doctor was fated to die in his (Jung's) stead. He warned his doctor to take care of himself, but the physician did not heed his patient's advice. On the same day that Jung was permitted to sit up in bed for the first time, his doctor came down with a fever and soon died of a septic infection.[22] Eleven years later, a synchronistic event occurred when the late doctor's brother, also a physician, sent Jung a card from the island of Kos. In a note of thanks, Jung told his doctor's brother about his vision. To the end of his life Jung maintained that premonitory events such as this one hint at the existence of another order of things lying behind the ordinary world of time and space, and prompt us to form our own image of what awaits us when *our* time comes to leave the earth.

Synchronicity

The experiences recounted in this chapter are examples of synchronicity, in which outer and inner events coincide in an acausal but meaningful way. Jaffé explains this phenomenon by pointing out that archetypes, which function as the organizing principle of synchronistic events, manifest on two levels—as objective physical events and as our inner psychic perceptions of those events. Normally the outer event and the inner perception happen simultaneously, but in premonitory experiences the two occur separately.[23] Jaffé suggests that we think of outer events and inner perceptions as separate facets of the same arche-type, connected by the "illuminating link" of meaning.[24] The strong emotion associated with the archetype of death may also be a factor in premonitory experiences, she writes.

If the split between an event and our perception of it occurs spatially, as in my friend's dream of saying goodbye to Barbara, we perceive the event at the time that it occurs, even though we are not physically present. If time is relativized, we foresee an event before it actually occurs, as in Elena's dream of the light on the monitor screen. In some cases death is not mentioned directly, as in Jung's dream of talking to his father about marital psychology; in other dreams it is depicted in archetypal images, as in my dream of the horses and Jung's dream of the Wild Huntsman. If we can put aside our predilection for causal thinking and learn to think about synchronistic events as acausal psychic/physical manifestations of a single archetype, we can open ourselves to the possibility of meaning in these events.

Summary

To summarize, premonitory dreams share certain common features:

1. The dream connections usually exist between people who are linked by strong emotional and psychological bonds.
2. The dreams often occur when the dreamer and the person dreamed about are physically separated, even by a great distance. The emotional bond between the two people appears to be more powerful than the spatial distance between them.
3. Although the dreamer may not know it at the time, the dream may occur at the exact moment of an accident or death.
4. Many premonitory dreams deal with unfinished business between the dreamer and the person dreamed about. Themes of forgiveness and farewell are frequently present.
5. Archetypal images and symbols convey the numinous quality of the thin time and space between this world and the next.
6. Finally, such dreams seem to serve as a preparation for the "painful blow of fate" that is about to fall, even though nothing can be done to prevent it. Dreamers report that the sense of meaning in these warnings makes devastating losses somewhat easier to bear.

But what comes next? As Jung put it, "a human being is torn away from us, and what remains is the icy stillness of death."[25] He experienced that stillness after his wife's death, but later dreamed that she was continuing her studies of the Grail in the south of France. Much later, she appeared to him in a striking vision of beauty and wholeness. The tension between these opposites—the icy stillness of death and the vivid dream images of the dead—characterizes the thin time following the death of a loved one. Just when we are adjusting to their absence from the physical world, the dead reappear in dreams with all the energy and vigor of life. This paradox, which informs the initial period of mourning, is the focus of the next chapter.

Notes

1 C. G. Jung, *Memories*, 333.
2 C. G. Jung, *C. G. Jung Speaking*, 463.
3 C. G. Jung, *Memories*, 336.
4 *Ibid.*, 331.
5 *Ibid.*, 334.
6 *Ibid.*
7 *Ibid.*, 335–336.
8 *Ibid.*, 336–344.
9 *Ibid.*, 346–347.

10 G. Mogenson, *Greeting the Angels*, 110. Jung's essay, "Marriage as a Psychological Relationship," can be found in *CW* Vol. 17, *The Development of Personality*.
11 C. G. Jung, *Memories*, 344–345.
12 *Ibid.*, 345.
13 *Ibid.*, 346.
14 A. Jaffé, Introduction to C. G. Jung, *Memories*, 7.
15 A. Jaffé, *Apparitions*, 130.
16 *Ibid.*, 43.
17 *Ibid.*, 32.
18 V. Kast, *A Time to Mourn*, 21–28.
19 *Ibid.*, 29.
20 G. Grubbs, *Bereavement Dreaming and the Individuating Soul*, 52–56.
21 *Ibid.*
22 Jung's account of this experience can be found in *Memories*, 320–324.
23 A. Jaffé, *Apparitions*, 192.
24 *Ibid.*, 193.
25 C. G. Jung, *Memories*, 346.

Chapter 4

"Let your tears fertilize my ground"

The gift of tears

In the days following Elizabeth's funeral I felt exhausted, like a convalescent recovering from a major illness. Tears were close to the surface, but still I could not cry. Then, a few days after I dropped the wilted flowers into the river, I had this dream:

> I am grieving and wishing that I could hug Elizabeth again. Then all of a sudden she is there and I *am* hugging her. She is wearing the dark red sweater I had made for her father before we were married. I can feel her body clearly, her ribs against my arms and her strong arms around me. I am crying and laughing at the same time because I am so glad to see her and touch her again. As we embrace, she says to me, "Let your tears fertilize my ground." Then she is gone and I wake up.

In this dream I knew that Elizabeth was dead, and yet she seemed utterly real and very much alive. I could see her, hear her, embrace her, almost smell her. She did not feel like a ghost, but a fully embodied being. Our hug was as warm as the many we had shared during her lifetime. The contrast between the reality of her death and the sense of her vivid presence was jarring, and her words at the end of the dream were baffling. "Let your tears fertilize my ground"—what could that possibly mean? I didn't know, but as I woke up, the brittle shell around my heart finally cracked and I wept for a long time. It was a relief to be able to feel again, even though the feelings were excruciating. The implication of Elizabeth's message seemed to be that if I would let myself cry, my tears would water her "ground" and engender new life there. I had no idea what she meant, but I held her words close to my heart.

The stages of grief

Before commenting further on this dream, I want to place it in the context of the so-called "stages of grief." I was familiar with much of the literature on grief because I had written my M.S.W. thesis on the subject in 1975. At that time I had suffered several losses, including the death of my mother, and I hoped that studying grief would ease my way through the process of mourning. I started with Dr. Elisabeth Kubler-Ross's now-famous study *On Death and Dying.*[1] Based on conversations with terminally patients at the University of Chicago's teaching hospital, Kubler-Ross identified the five "stages" of denial, anger, bargaining, depression, and acceptance. Later she noted that people suffering other major losses, including bereavement, often experience the same stages. My dream of Elizabeth came as the first stage, denial, was giving way to a long period of inner turmoil marked by sadness, anger, depression, guilt, and many other emotions. I never went through the "bargaining" stage with either Elizabeth or my mother, because they were gone and there was no way to win them back. I think that the stage of "acceptance" will always be a work in progress.

Other writers who studied the topic of grief before Kubler-Ross had come to similar conclusions. In 1917, Sigmund Freud's "Mourning and Melancholia" distinguished simple grief from "melancholia," which would be described today as a major depressive disorder. Freud observed that those in mourning exhibit "a profoundly painful depression, a loss of interest in the outside world, the loss of the ability to love, [and] the inhibition of any kind of performance."[2] He suggests that mourning involves gradual detachment of libido (psychic energy) from the dead and the "decathecting" (emotional release) of each painful memory. At last the bereaved decide to live again, rather than joining their loved ones in death, and become "free and uninhibited" and ready to form a new attachment.[3]

Years after Freud's work, other psychologists elaborated on his model. Melanie Klein observed that mourning reactivates the "depressive position" of infant development, along with its characteristic emotions of guilt, anger, and sorrow.[4] John Bowlby, a pioneer in attachment theory, observed infants who had been separated from their mothers during the London Blitz in World War II. These children responded to the trauma of separation in three distinct emotional phases: protest, emotional disorganization, and reorganization.[5] Another British writer, Colin Parkes, studied delayed grief in twenty-one psychiatric patients and concluded that grief is a form of separation anxiety, with pining for the lost loved one its most salient feature. Those who suffer from it are predisposed to clinical depression, he noted.[6] Jung did not write a specific essay on grief, but reference to it runs throughout his work and is cited many times in this book.

After Elizabeth's death I did not need another dry, clinical study of the stages of grief, but a warm-blooded human account of the experience of mourning. I also needed help understanding my dreams, but I found few references to grief dreams in the clinical literature. (Fortunately, since that time many books on mourning and grief dreams have appeared, many of which are cited here.) As my own mourning proceeded, I realized that the "stages of grief" do not occur in the neat, orderly sequence implied by the literature. Instead of following one another in a straight line, the "stages" are jumbled up and occur at random or even simultaneously. My experience as a therapist corroborated this observation. I had worked with many bereaved people but had never seen any of them progress through grief in a linear step-by-step fashion. One day (or minute) they would be in denial; the next moment they would be crying, exploding in anger, voicing guilt and regret, even laughing as they recounted a humorous memory of their loved one. Then they would suddenly revert to denial and exclaim, "It just can't be true! I still can't believe it!" After many months and many painful repetitions of this cycle, a glimmer of acceptance would finally begin to dawn—but at first it was evanescent. Even when it appeared more often, a deep sadness lingered and was gradually absorbed into the bereaved person's psychic structure. My own mental picture of this process now, more than thirty years after Elizabeth's death, is an image of a drop of blood (like the one in my premonitory dream) falling into a transparent glass bowl of clear water. At first the scarlet droplet is noticeable as it penetrates the surface and begins to swirl around in the liquid. But gradually the tiny drop is absorbed into the water until its presence can no longer be detected. Even a taste of the water would not reveal the distinctive iron flavor of blood. And yet blood is present in the new solution. It has dissolved so thoroughly that it can no longer be distinguished from the water. To switch metaphors, I also imagine grief as a long voyage in a fragile ship on a turbulent sea. Rolling waves alternate with spells of uneasy calm and moments of unexpected peace. When waves of emotion strike with gale force, the only way to survive is to tie everything down, hold tight, and hope to ride out the storm.

While working on the material that would become my first book, I discovered Joan Didion's book *The Year of Magical Thinking*, written after her husband's sudden death from a heart attack. Here was the first-person account I had needed in my first year of grief, written in Didion's stark, evocative prose. Describing her own plunge into grief, she observes, "Grief comes in waves, paroxysms, sudden apprehensions that weaken the knees and blind the eyes and obliterate the dailiness of life. Virtually everyone who has ever experienced grief mentions this phenomenon of 'waves.' "[7] She also describes what she calls the "the vortex effect," which suggests water swirling down a drain, a tornado swooping down from the sky, or a hurricane spinning ashore and wreaking destruction.[8] A vortex is a torrent of emotion triggered by an unexpected stimulus associated with the dead loved one. It might also be described as a PTSD reaction. Didion's experiences of being pulled into a vortex included glimpsing the theater where she and her husband had seen the film *The Graduate* many years before, and finding on his desk a faintly penciled list of the characters who had died in his most recent novel. In my own experience, it did not take much to spawn a wave or sweep me into a vortex. The smallest thing could do it: a song Elizabeth had liked, a photograph I had not seen before, the sound of her voice on an old tape recording. During the early weeks of grief, the waves and vortexes were relentless. As time passed, their intensity and frequency diminished. But still they came. Years after her death a vortex sucked me in when I discovered one of her long blonde hairs on an old black sweater. Parting with her computer spawned another vortex. It took a long time to "decathect" each memory, to use Freud's terminology. Even now, an unexpected reminder can trigger a wave. For example, recently one of Elizabeth's high school friends sent me some photos she had taken more than thirty years ago. I had seen some of them before, but many were new to me. All of a sudden there was my daughter, eternally young, lying in a bed of flowers, her blonde hair spread out like a halo on the ground. I was not surprised when a wave of sadness and nostalgia washed over me, but the image of the bed of flowers took my breath away. They reminded me of the flowers strewn on Elizabeth's grave, the wilted flowers I had dropped into the river a few days after her funeral, and even the flowers that might spring from her "ground," fertilized with my tears. Here was another synchronicity, a linking of events and images that seemed more than coincidental.

The myth of Demeter and Persephone

In the ancient Greek myth of Demeter, the goddess of fertility and the grain, and her daughter Persephone, I found another tale of mourning that spoke to my soul. I had learned the myth in a high school Latin class, where it was interpreted as a metaphor for the cycle of the seasons—the death of vegetative life in winter and its re-emergence from the earth in spring. The myth came to light again during my training at the Jung Institute, where classical mythology is understood as an expression of psychological processes in symbolic, archetypal form. I do not remember exactly when it happened, but not long after Elizabeth's death the penny dropped and I realized that this myth of a mother's loss of her daughter bore an uncanny resemblance to my own experience. To begin with, the coal-black steeds that carried Persephone down to the underworld reminded me of the strange horses that led Elizabeth into oblivion in my premonitory dream. I could also see that the myth's dramatic structure—Demeter's initial shock, her search for her daughter, her attempt to immortalize another child, her implacable anger, and her eventual compromise with Hades—closely follows the pattern of the stages of grief. In the myth, the experience of loss is portrayed in poetic language and archetypal images rather than in sterile clinical terms. And so the tale became a map that guided me out of numbness and denial, through years of emotional turmoil, and towards a degree of acceptance.

There are many versions of the Greek myth of "fair-tressed" Demeter and her "slim-ankled" daughter.[9] The following composite draws upon several sources to tell a story of loss, grief, and transformation:

> Once upon a time Hades, dark-haired Lord of the Underworld, spies a beautiful maiden, Persephone, gathering flowers in a green field, and instantly falls in love with her. He asks his brother Zeus, the king of the gods and the girl's father, for her hand in marriage, but Zeus, knowing that her mother Demeter will never forgive him if he agrees, neither gives nor withholds his consent. Not to be denied, Hades seizes Persephone and carries her off in his chariot drawn by four coal-black horses. She cries out to her father for

help, but Zeus does not answer. Then Hades commands the earth to open and carries the screaming girl into his underworld kingdom.

At that moment Demeter hears her daughter's cry and feels a sharp pain in her heart. She tears her garments, refuses food and drink, will not bathe, and cannot rest. For nine days she wanders the earth, a flaming torch in each hand, searching for her daughter—but no one can tell her where Persephone has gone. On the tenth day the goddess Hecate, associated with crossroads, magic, and ghosts, joins her and they consult the Sun, who has seen the abduction and tells them the truth.

When she learns her daughter's fate, Demeter is overcome with grief and rage. Leaving Mt. Olympus, she disguises her beauty, takes the form of an old woman, and wanders for a long time through earthly cities and fields. At last she comes to Eleusis and rests near the Maiden's Well, where she meets the daughters of the king and agrees to serve as a nurse for their infant brother. Still bowed down with grief, she tries to immortalize the child by anointing him with ambrosia and placing him each night in the fire like a log. When his mother protests, Demeter flies into a rage, snatches the child from the fire, and pronounces his fate. In one version of the story he becomes the founder of games of war; in another he dies; in a third he grows up to teach men the arts of cultivation. Then Demeter reveals herself as a goddess, commands the king to build a shrine in her honor, and institutes the Mysteries of Eleusis.

The king builds the shrine and Demeter moves into it, but still she pines for her lost daughter. In her wrath she brings a deadly drought upon the earth so that grain ceases to grow, threatening the human race with extinction. Finally Zeus sends his personal messenger, Iris, to parlay with Demeter, who pays no heed. Then he dispatches all the gods to plead with her, but she refuses to restore the earth until she sees her daughter again. As a last resort, Zeus sends Hermes, messenger to all the gods, to negotiate with Hades, who agrees to let Persephone return to her mother. But before he lets her go, he gives Persephone a pomegranate seed to eat, thus assuring that she will have to return to him for part of every year. Hermes escorts her back to earth, where she and Demeter have a joyful reunion. But from now on she must divide her time between the Underworld and Olympus. After Zeus and Rhea, the mother of the gods, ratify the compromise, Demeter restores the bounty of the earth. Then she and her daughter ascend to Olympus, where they are held in eternal reverence.

A crack in the universe

In the myth of Demeter and Persephone, the first stage of grief begins when Demeter hears her daughter's cry and a sharp pain pierces her heart. When my son called me with the news of his sister's death, I felt that sharp pain myself. To paraphrase Joan Didion, life as I knew it ended in the instant.[10] Years later

I heard a lecture in which Gilles Quispel, an expert on the Gnostic gospels, used the phrase "a crack in the universe."[11] That was exactly it. The universe, which had seemed solid and orderly, had cracked open, revealing a bottomless abyss into which Elizabeth had fallen. Jung evokes this experience when he writes that death is a "fearful piece of brutality" in which "all the bridges have been smashed at one blow."[12]

When Demeter feels that blow, she tears off her headdress, throws down her veil, and refuses to eat, drink, or bathe. Then she wanders the earth for nine days, searching for her lost daughter. Her behavior reflects the emotional paralysis of early grief, when the bereaved literally or symbolically rend their garments and neglect basic activities such as eating, drinking, bathing, and dressing. In a book written after the suicide of her son, Charlotte Mathes observes that the tearing of garments symbolizes the emotional dismemberment suffered by the recently bereaved. For example, the Jewish mourning rite of *keriah* re-enacts Jacob's rending of his garments when he sees Joseph's torn, bloody coat and believes that his son is dead. Rather than tearing an entire garment, the bereaved tear or cut a black ribbon or piece of cloth and pin it to their clothing to express their torn emotional state.[13] In this initial period of shock, the body reacts as if to a physical trauma. The heart rate quickens or becomes irregular, body temperature drops, breathing becomes shallow and painful, and digestion is unsettled. Sleep, if it comes at all, is restless and fitful. Or it becomes a temporary escape into the oblivion of unconsciousness.

In this stage of grief, we know that our loved one is dead but we still feel an uncanny sense of their presence. We may imagine that we see them walking down the street, driving past in a car, or disappearing around a corner. We pine and search for them, all the while knowing that we will not find them. The line between fact and fantasy is blurred and we do not feel solidly grounded in reality. It requires enormous effort to make a simple decision (such as what to eat for breakfast or whether to eat breakfast at all), to put one foot in front of the other, or even to get out of bed in the morning. It is almost impossible to feel, think, move, or act. Numbness and denial are ever-present (and not entirely unwelcome) companions. But of course, we cannot stay numb forever. Sooner or later the fog of denial lifts and painful emotions begin to break through. In the myth of Demeter this happens when the Sun finally reveals that Hades has abducted Persephone and carried her into the underworld. Upon hearing this news, the goddess leaves Olympus, descends to the earth, and enters the world of time, space, and mortality. She feels the human emotions of grief and rage, perhaps for the first time. At that moment she plunges into the underworld of mourning just as precipitously as Persephone had plunged into Hades.

"Metapsychic" dreams

I was in the initial stage of grief when I had the dream of embracing Elizabeth and hearing her tell me to let my tears fertilize her ground. I held that dream in my heart for months, savoring the memory of her presence but puzzling over the meaning of her words. When I eventually returned to Zürich to resume my training, I scoured the library for books that might help me understand the special quality of my dream. One day I happened upon a diploma thesis by Emmanuel X. Kennedy, "The Alchemy of Death," which finally shed light upon the special quality of my dream. In his paper Kennedy coins the term "metapsychic" to describe dreams in which

> images of the dead appear with certain attributes. They are of a numinous nature with a vivid, crystal-clear 'photographic' objectivity. As in the case of archetypal dreams,... they remain fresh in the memory, even for decades. They usually have an intense emotional impact on the dreamer and are characterized furthermore by a unique, indescribable feeling tone—a touch of eternity.[14]

Something "clicked" when I read this passage because Kennedy could have been describing my own dream. As I read his thesis, I realized that vivid dreams of the dead constitute a specific category of dream experience. He continues,

> We don't make our dreams, they happen to us... The idea—prevalent even among psycho-analysts that "we are makers of our dreams; our unconscious makes them" is not only fallacious but even dangerous: for what we have then is an inflated, egocentric individual who identifies with... [the unconscious], which is infinitely larger and more powerful than the tiny ego.[15]

This passage made sense to me because I knew that my "tiny ego" could never have created my dream's vibrant reality or invented Elizabeth's mysterious words. I could not explain the dream away as a wish-fulfillment, a compensatory fantasy, or a figment of my imagination. It was another sort of dream altogether, and Kennedy had found the words to define it. His validation of my own experience was immensely reassuring. I knew that I was not crazy, that my dream was not a hallucination, and above all, that I was not alone.

Geri Grubbs, whose book is cited in the previous chapter, is another Jungian analyst who has written about grief dreams. She coined the term "transliminal" to refer to dreams which are marked by a powerful transcendent quality and a feeling that the dead are objectively present. In such dreams, she writes, the image of the deceased often functions as "a spirit guide to the bereaved's recovery from grief and in... [his or her] individuation process."[16] Unfortunately, her book had not been written when I was grieving Elizabeth's death. But when I discovered it years later, it offered further corroboration of Kennedy's findings and my own experience. In fact, in my first dream Elizabeth had already begun to function as a guide, assuring me of her spiritual presence and opening my mind and heart to a new understanding of death and rebirth.

Three dream images

As I examined my dream's three central symbols—the dark red sweater, the fertilizing tears, and the image of "my ground"—a meaningful pattern of personal and archetypal meaning gradually began to emerge. The red sweater was one that I had knitted for Elizabeth's father before our marriage. I think of it now as a transitional object that connected us while I was an undergraduate and he was in graduate school, hundreds of miles away. Years later, when our marriage unraveled, I lost track of the sweater and assumed that he no longer had it. I almost forgot about it until Elizabeth's teenage years, when she grew tall and began to "borrow" her father's clothes. Then she wore it often, as though to remind herself (and us) that our family bond, tattered and frayed though it might be, had not disintegrated altogether. The sweater's dark red color reminded me of the spot of blood on the sand in my premonitory dream and also of the blood which Elizabeth shed at her death. It suggested that "blood ties" between family members endure, even in the aftermath of divorce and death.

The next image, the fertilizing tears, implies that the tears of grief are also the water of life. As I researched the symbol of tears, I discovered a book by Loring M. Danforth and Alexander Tsiaras entitled *The Death Rituals of Rural Greece*, an account of the authors' visit to several Greek villages where ancient mourning rituals were still observed. In that rural culture, tears of grief were believed to nourish the flowers placed on graves and to "bring comfort to the world of the dead because they represent contact and communication with the world of the living."[17] For example, the authors quote a lament in which "the singer expresses the hope that the tears she sheds will actually resurrect the deceased."[18] In another lament the singer prays

> that the tears become a cool spring, a lake, an ocean,
> and flood down into the underworld;
> so that the unwashed can wash, and the thirsty can drink;
> so that good housewives can knead and bake bread;
> so that handsome young men can comb and part their hair
> when they want to go for a walk, when they want to go out for a stroll;
> and so that little children in school can make ink to write.[19]

Other cultures also believed in the healing property of tears. In China the tears of grief were thought to ensure the soul's passage from this world to the next. On the seventh day after a death, relatives would rise early to make offerings and weep, believing that if they wept for the deceased before he knew that he had died, his sorrow would be diminished. "The more we weep, the less he must," they said.[20] In ancient Babylon, ritual weeping for the death of the fertility god accompanied the annual sowing of the grain and ensured that the crops would sprout each spring.[21] Ancient Egyptians believed that the rains causing the Nile to overflow its banks each year, providing essential nutrients for the crops, consisted of the tears of Isis shed for her dead husband, Osiris. It was believed that the gods' tears for Osiris were distilled into embalming fluid, which conferred divine powers on his dead body.[22] In her book *On Dreams and Death*, Marie-Louise von Franz includes an ancient image of an attendant watering the body of Osiris while new shoots of grain sprout from his corpse.[23]

Two biblical passages also came to my mind in connection with the image of tears fertilizing the earth. In the Old Testament, Psalm 126:5–6 declares,

> They that sow in tears shall reap in joy.
> He that goeth forth and weepeth, bearing precious seed,
> Shall doubtless come with rejoicing, bringing his sheaves with him.[24]

In the New Testament Gospel of John, Jesus says, "except a corn of wheat fall into the ground and die, it abideth alone: but if it die, it bringeth forth much fruit" (John 12:24).[25] Both passages refer to the literal death of the seed, but also to the death of an old orientation to life which must die so that a new one can be born. The psalm even implies that the "precious seed" will not grow without life-giving "tears and weeping." In bereavement, the seed symbolizes the physical relationship with the deceased, which must die in order for a new spiritual relationship to grow and "bear much fruit."

In my dream the possibility of new life springing from the death of the old is implied in Elizabeth's words, "fertilize my ground." Somehow she is aware that the tears of grief will fertilize the ground of the psyche and bring forth new psychological and spiritual life. The word "ground" reminded me of Paul Tillich's elusive metaphor for God, "the ground of being," by which he meant the source and foundation of all life.[26] He was not referring to the literal earth under our feet, but to the cosmic underpinnings of life itself. In the dream Elizabeth uses the phrase "*my* ground" very specifically, as if to distinguish it from any other person's ground. I took this to mean that my tears of grief could give new life to her unique essence, even after her ashes had been buried in the earth. As Greg Mogenson states in *Greeting the Angels*, "the actual work of mourning is a matter as individual as the loss itself… The most important variable of the mourning process, regardless of the 'stage' the bereaved appear to be in, is the identity of the deceased."[27] My dream came two weeks after Elizabeth's death, when I was just beginning to face the reality of her loss. It was the first in a series of reunion dreams, a type that occurs frequently in the course of bereavement. As we "greet the angels" of the dead in these dreams, we are confronted with a conundrum. We know that our loved ones are dead, and yet they seem very much alive in our dreams. The next chapter explores the paradoxical aspect of reunion dreams, beginning with a dream of my own and then considering dreams told by Jung, Freud, von Franz, and others.

Notes

1 E. Kubler-Ross, *On Death and Dying*.
2 S. Freud, "Mourning and Melancholia," 311.
3 *Ibid.*, 312.
4 M. Klein, "Mourning and its Relation to Manic-Depressive States," 125–153.
5 J. Bowlby, "Grief and Mourning in Infancy and Early Childhood," 9–52.
6 C. M. Parkes, *Bereavement: Studies of Grief in Adult Life*.
7 J. Didion, *The Year of Magical Thinking*, 27.
8 *Ibid.*, 107.
9 Homer, "Hymn to Demeter," 4. My retelling of the story is a composite based upon Crudden's translation and incorporating elements from: Thomas Bulfinch, *Bulfinch's Mythology* (New York: Avenel Books, 1978); James G. Frazer, *The Golden Bough* (New York: Avenel Books, 1981); and Robert Graves, *The Greek Myths*, Vol. 1 (Baltimore, MD: Penguin Books, 1955).
10 J. Didion, *The Year of Magical Thinking*, 3.
11 G. Quispsel, lecture given at the C. G. Jung Institute, Zürich, in the late 1980s or early 1990s.
12 C. G. Jung, *Memories*, 346.
13 C. Mathes, *And a Sword Shall Pierce Your Heart*, 45–46.
14 E. X. Kennedy, "The Alchemy of Death," 7.
15 *Ibid.*, 4.
16 G. Grubbs, *Bereavement Dreaming and the Individuating Soul*, 23.
17 L. M. Danforth and A. Tsiaras, *The Death Rituals of Rural Greece*, 110.
18 *Ibid.*
19 *Ibid.*, 111.
20 E. M. Ahern, *The Cult of the Dead in a Chinese Village*, 225.
21 A. De Vries, *Dictionary of Symbols and Imagery*, and G. Jobes, *Dictionary of Mythology, Folklore, and Symbols*.
22 S. Grof, *Books of the Dead: Manuals for Living and Dying*, 86.
23 M.-L. von Franz, *On Dreams and Death*, 11.
24 *The Holy Bible*, King James Version, 805.
25 *Ibid.*, 1387.
26 P. Tillich, *Systematic Theology*, Vol. I, 112.
27 G. Mogenson, *Greeting the Angels*, 101.

Chapter 5

"Touch me"

Reunion dreams

Pining and searching for the lost loved one is an instinctive reaction to the trauma of loss.[1] In the Homeric "Hymn to Demeter," the goddess "rushed like a bird in her search" for her lost daughter.[2] Driven by the same instinct, the Egyptian goddess Isis roamed up and down the Nile seeking her dead husband, Osiris. In the Babylonian Epic of Gilgamesh, the hero wandered the desert in pursuit of Enkidu, his lost soul-brother.[3] These ancient tales convey our longing to reunite with those we have lost. (Even the word "lost," often used as a euphemism for "dead," implies the possibility of reunion.) We know that they are dead, and yet we continue to pine and search for them. Then, just as we are beginning to accept that we will not find them, the longed-for reunion takes place in our dreams. Two weeks after my dream of the fertilizing tears I had another dream:

> Elizabeth and I are with a group of young people. I am the only one who can see and hear her. I am overjoyed to be with her again. She says, "Touch me," and I do. Her body feels solid and warm, not ghostly and insubstantial. She eats something, as if to show me that she still needs physical nourishment. She is happy and healthy and seems to be fine. Then the young people pile into a bus and she goes with them. The place where she sits looks empty to them, but somehow they know they can't sit there. They can't see her sitting in the "empty" place, but I can.

As noted before, the tension between presence and absence appears often in bereavement dreams. For example, my friend who dreamed of saying goodbye to her friend Barbara (see Chapter 3) also dreamed of her father soon after his death. He appeared in her kitchen and seemed as alive as ever, until she tried to touch him and found that her hand passed through him as through thin air. In the early days of grief, the dead seem to be both present and absent, real and unreal, here and not here. As my friend Terry, who was with me the night of Elizabeth's death (and who had recently lost his sister) put it succinctly, "They are very present in their absence." Films such as *Ghost* and *The Sixth Sense* and novels such as *The Lovely Bones* and *Lincoln in the Bardo* tell the stories of recently departed spirits who attempt to make contact with the living, with limited degrees of success. Two passages from the Gospel of John also convey the "touch me/do not touch me" contradiction. Immediately after his resurrection, Jesus says to Mary Magdalene, "Touch me not; for I am not yet ascended to my Father." But eight days later he says to Thomas, "Reach hither thy finger, and behold my hands; and reach hither thy hand, and thrust it into my side: and be not faithless, but believing."[4] Whether they appear in dreams, films, novels, or the Bible, images of the tangible yet intangible dead bring comfort, sorrow, and also confusion. The dream above, in which Elizabeth told me to touch her, had the numinous feeling-tone of our first dream reunion, and yet something had already begun to change. At first I could see and hear her and her body seemed warm and tangible. But then she moved away from me, got into a bus with some other young people, and started to become invisible. I could still see her, but the young people could not—as if to imply that it would soon be difficult for me to see her as well. Less than month after her death, her image was already becoming insubstantial.

Objective/subjective: reprise

In her book *On Dreams and Death*, Marie-Louise von Franz recounts a dream of her dead father which raises the issue of physical contact with the dead:

> I heard the doorbell ring and "knew" at once somehow that this was my father coming. I opened the door and there he stood with a suitcase. I remembered from *The Tibetan Book of the Dead* that people who died suddenly should be told that they are dead, but before I could say so he smiled at me and said: "Of course I know that I am dead, but may I not visit you?" I said, "Of course, come in," and then asked, "How are you now? Are you happy?"[5]

In his answer, which I will paraphrase here, von Franz's dream father says that "happy" means something different to the living than it does to the dead. He tells her that he is studying at the music academy in Vienna, which he had wanted to do all his life. He will not go into his former bedroom, saying that now he is only a guest. Then he tells her to leave the room and signals her not to embrace him, saying, "It is not good for either the dead or the living to be together too long."[6] As the dream ends, she thinks that she has forgotten to turn off the electric stove and worries that there is danger of fire. Then she wakes up, feeling hot and sweating.

Von Franz told this dream to Jung, who interpreted it "on the objective level, that is, as a dream concerning my real father."[7] Jung viewed the overheated stove and the hot, sweaty feeling as "a healing defense against the danger of contagion by the chill of death."[8] In her summary of the dream, von Franz states that she understood its message to be that *"the world of the living and the world of the dead should not come too close to each other, that they are somehow dangerous for each other."*[9] In other words, the "chill of death" can be dangerous for the living, but is offset in the dream by the image of the hot stove and her increased body temperature. Since death is not physically contagious, the "contagion" must be of another kind. Von Franz notes that her dream father exhibits unusual emotional "chilliness" by insisting that he is "only a guest," refusing to go into his former bedroom, and refraining from embracing her. She infers that this emotional detachment is dangerous because it might "infect" the living with the same coldness. But how can contact with the living be dangerous for the dead? Von Franz does not elaborate on this aspect of the question, but perhaps contact with the living might be too "warm" for the dead, keeping them too emotionally attached to their loved ones. The idea that the living and the dead continue to affect one another will be explored at greater length in the following chapters.

Von Franz emphasizes that Jung interpreted her dream objectively, as though it referred to her "real" father, but interpretation on the subjective level might have been fruitful as well. For example, the dream father might represent von Franz's father complex, which had been activated by her father's death, and was now cautioning her to keep a safe distance from "him." Her warm body temperature at the end of the dream might indicate that father issues were a "hot topic" for her and that she needed to cool down her emotional response to them.

In another example of the objective/subjective distinction, von Franz discusses a case in which a fellow analyst consulted her about the dreams of a young woman whose fiancé had died in an airplane accident. Von Franz's colleague interpreted the dream figure of the fiancé subjectively, as an image of the dreamer's animus, or masculine side—an interpretation with which von Franz concurred, with the exception of six dreams in which she felt that the dream image might represent the dead man himself. Her colleague requested a consultation with Jung, who (without knowing von Franz's choice) "picked out the same six dreams and interpreted them on the objective level." In conclusion, von Franz observes that we "can 'feel' whether the figure of a dead person in a dream is being used as a symbol for some inner reality or whether it 'really' represents the dead." This "feeling" occurs when "interpretation on the subjective level makes little or no sense, even though the dream has a strong numinous effect."[10]

In my "touch me" dream, the figure of Elizabeth did not "feel" like "a symbol for some inner reality." Subjective interpretation of her image as an aspect of my own personality made "little or no sense" to me. But an objective interpretation provided meaningful insights on my relationship with Elizabeth both before and after her death. In the first section of the dream, her image was vivid and substantial. I could see her, hear her, talk to her, and touch her, just as I could when she was alive. She even ate something, as if to demonstrate that she was not a disembodied spirit. This part of the dream pictured my relationship with Elizabeth before her death, when we used to talk, embrace, and enjoy meals together. But then the scene changed and she left me. She got into a vehicle and prepared to go on a trip with a group of young people. The dream did not identify them, but they seemed to be a group of fellow travelers. My association was that they might represent other young people who had recently died and were leaving their bodily life behind. When Elizabeth joined them, her place seemed "empty" but somehow they knew she was there. It was as though she was making the transition to another level of reality beyond visible, audible, and tangible form. This part of the dream hinted at the changing nature of my relationship with Elizabeth after her death. Although I could still "see" her, the dream suggested that our relationship was moving from a literal, physical connection to an intangible, imaginal one.

It is possible to interpret dreams such as this one as evidence of ongoing contact between the living and the dead. Jung leans in this direction in his comments on his own dreams, as he did with von Franz's dream of her father. Then, in the next sentence, he often hastens to add that there is no way to verify the reality of the afterlife or the postmortem existence of disembodied spirits. The tension between these two positions runs throughout his work. My own view is that since we cannot know whether the spirits of the dead do (or do not) exist, it is best to keep an open mind. All we know for certain is that images of the dead appear in the dreams of the bereaved, and that these dream appearances can be deeply meaningful. Jung tends to adopt an "either/or" standpoint with respect to the subjective versus objective interpretation of dreams. According to this approach, the dream image of Elizabeth would represent *either* an aspect of my own psyche (the subjective view) *or* Elizabeth herself as she now exists in the "afterlife" (the objective inter-pretation). This position creates problems, however. First of all, dream images often have both a subjective and an objective significance at the same time. For example, von Franz's dream father might represent *both* an aspect of her person-ality *and* her actual father as he existed in another dimension. Holding the two perspectives side by side, rather than eliminating one in favor of the other, can produce some valuable insights. Second, in adopting the objective approach, Jung often equates dream images of the dead with their actual existence in the hereafter. Since the reality of the afterlife cannot be verified, this position may be meaning-less to the "doubting Thomases" among us who need physical evidence to confirm our beliefs. But there is another way to interpret dream images of the dead, and that is to regard them as psychic facts, figures that now exist on the imaginal rather than the physical level.

The imaginal level

The term "imaginal" was coined by Henri Corbin, a French scholar of Islam, to denote the realm of images. Sufi mystics, writes Corbin, believed that between

> the empirical world and the world of abstract understanding" there exists "an intermediate world,… the world of the Image,… a world as ontologically real

as the world of the senses and the world of the intellect, a world that requires a faculty of perception belonging to it.

Corbin calls that faculty "the imaginative power" and states that it is a cognitive function "as fully real as the faculties of sensory perception or intellectual intuition." It is not to be confused with fantasy, which "produces only the 'imaginary.'"[11] In other words, it is not the same as wishing, pretending, or daydreaming. Although it is a cognitive function, it does not originate with the ego. The imaginal realm has an independent, autonomous quality and is unrelated to the images we hold in our personal memory-bank. To my knowledge Jung does not use the word "imaginal" in his writing, but his terms "objective psyche" and "collective unconscious" refer to the same reality. Whatever term we use, we are speaking of a level that exists beyond the scope of the five senses and the rational intellect, but reveals itself in art, literature, mythology, and dreams.

Greg Mogenson describes the imaginal realm in his discussion of two types of dreams that occur in mourning. The first type emphasizes the grief of the bereaved and "focus[es] on the *attachment relationship* between the bereaved survivor and the lost loved one *as the lost loved one was known historically*."[12] The second type

> explore[s] the on-going imaginal life of the lost love-object... The lost love-object appears in a novel aspect. In the imaginal world of the dream it lives, moves, and has its being in a manner quite indifferent to the grief of the bereaved.[13]

The distinction between the two types is crucial in the interpretation of bereavement dreams and in tracing the evolution of the mourning process.

Verena Kast observes that in reunion dreams the dreamer "often meets again with the deceased, who seems to be 'alive' and even healthy. The dreamer is aware, however, that he is dealing with someone who has died and knows also that they must part again."[14] She presents several dreams to illustrate this paradox, including one cited by Colin Parkes, as recorded in his book, *Bereavement: Studies in Grief in Adult Life*:

> He [the dreamer's husband] was in his coffin with the lid off and all of a sudden he came to life and got out. And I was so overjoyed to think that he was here that when I woke up I wondered where I was. It was so clear I was crying and laughing. I looked at him and he opened his mouth. I said, "He's alive. He's alive." I thought "Thank God, I'll have him to talk to."[15]

This dream contains features of both of Mogenson's "types": it focuses on the grief of the bereaved widow, but also explores the ongoing imaginal life of her deceased husband. In a similar dream Elena, whose boyfriend, George, had died of a heart attack (see Chapter 3), dreamed that he was lying in his coffin, but then began to move around and rub his eyes. She was "greatly cheered" when he saw her, greeted her, and talked to her. Later in the dream, they went for a walk and she noted that their relationship had changed greatly. Now "I experience him as if he were a part of me," she said.[16] As Mogenson observes, "a dream may juggle both concerns—grief *and* elegy, sentimentality *and* vision, remembered impressions *and* the 'images that yet / Fresh images beget.' "[17]

Dream encounters such as these may lead the dreamer to question deeply held attitudes and beliefs concerning life after death. Dualistic "either/or" thinking may evolve into what Romantic poet John Keats called "Negative Capability, that is when man is capable of being in uncertainties, Mysteries, doubts, without any irritable reaching after fact & reason."[18]

Fact and reason are important, but the transformative work of mourning invites us to live into the questions[19] raised by the death of someone close to us. In that work, we will ask our own questions and search for our own answers. By maintaining an open attitude to the "Mysteries," we honor our relationship with the dead and enlarge our own capacity for imaginative reflection.

More dream visits with Elizabeth

Not long after my "Touch me" dream, another dream repeated the theme of touching:

> I am with Elizabeth and am touching her, especially her arms. I feel amazed that she is real and that I can touch her. I want to tell people about this and show them how real she is. Then we are sitting in the rocking chair we sat in when she was a baby. She is sitting in my lap facing me as she used to do when she was little. In "real life" this would not be possible, but in the dream it is not a problem. It feels wonderful to hold her and rock her again.

In this dream I was aware that Elizabeth had died, but the joy of touching her eclipsed any feeling of sadness. Once again, she seemed absolutely real, with a warm, healthy body that showed no traces of the injuries she had sustained. When I woke up, the reality of her death struck me and another wave of tears began. But this time, as the wave subsided, I picked up my journal and began to write. Elizabeth had not spoken in the dream, but now the ears of my psyche (Corbin's "imaginative power") "heard" her tell me, in no uncertain terms, that I had work to do, which involved writing. As I wrote down her words, I asked myself, "Is this a wish-fulfillment or a visitation? A figment of my imagination or a 'real' message from Elizabeth?" I wanted to believe the latter, but there was no way to know for sure. One thing was certain, however: both the dream and Elizabeth's "message" were psychic facts. They really happened and it was my job to decide what to make of them. In my studies at the Institute I had been reading the work of Margaret Mahler on early childhood development.[20] I imagined that just as a child needs to return to her mother for "emotional refueling" during times of transition, Elizabeth might need to touch me again before moving on to whatever was next for her. I know that *I* needed to touch *her* again before I could undertake the task she had set for me. She was very direct in her message about writing, as if to emphasize that finding words for my inner experience would be an essential part of mourning for me.

As weeks and months passed, I had several more dreams in which Elizabeth was alive again or had survived the accident. In one dream she had not died but had just been in hiding for ten months. I reacted with joy and relief, but also with anger that she had allowed us to think that she was dead. This dream was full of emotion, but it also moved beyond personal affect into the space where imaginal figures "exist" quite apart from our daily concerns. As I began to feel that Elizabeth's dream image was finding its place in my inner world, my intense affective responses gradually abated and I grew curious about what might happen in her next dream appearance.

In *Mourning Unlived Lives: A Psychological Study of Childbearing Loss*, Jungian analyst Judith Savage observes that the process of mourning gradually loosens a mother's bond to her external child and replaces it with a relationship to the child's image. "Once this inner image is accepted as having a reality of its own," she writes, "it can then serve as a mediator to the unconscious of the survivor."[21] As the first anniversary of Elizabeth's death approached, her dream image began to function as a mediator to the unconscious for me. One dream from this period emphasized the distinction between "inside" and "outside" reality:

Elizabeth is here, very bright and alive, beautiful and smiling, with her long blonde hair flying out behind her. She doesn't speak, but somehow I get the message that now she can "be" on the inside only, not on the outside. In the dream, the words "inside" and "outside" refer to the interior and exterior of a house, but I realize that they also refer to the inner world of psyche and the outer world of objective reality.

Dream images of houses often refer one's inner home, the symbolic dwelling place of psyche. In my dream it is clear that the words "inside" and "outside" refer to the interior and exterior of a house, implying that Elizabeth now lives in my inner "house," although she no longer exists "outside." And yet she is more than a psychological introject or an inner object. As Mogenson points out,

it is not simply that at death our loved ones become incorporated into us. We become incorporated into them. The dead present the imagination in its purest psychic form. It is not that we grant them a semblance of eternal life by holding them in our memories. We imagine by means of them in accordance with the way they structure the imagination with their images. We are created in their likeness."[22]

Two days after the "house" dream came a dream in which Elizabeth "structure[d my] imagination" with a playful and animating image:

> Elizabeth blows on me, as if to say, "Look! I am alive! I still have breath!" I reciprocate playfully by blowing back on her. There is something humorous about this exchange of breath, as though we are teasing and playing with each other.

In this dream the connection between the living and the dead appears in the image of breath, a symbol of the energy that inspires all living beings. In the Book of Genesis, Adam does not come to life until God breathes the breath of life into his nostrils.[23] As if to demonstrate that she is very much alive in the imaginal world, Elizabeth breathes on me and fills me with her energy. When I breathe back on her, I animate her as a soul image. The exchange is mutual, joyful, and playful. Without this sort of play, the dead remain imaginally inanimate and the living are mired in what Mogenson calls "wallowing grief," stuck in memories of the past.[24] But when the dead come out of hiding, embrace us, even breathe on us, they invite us to live, work, and play with them in the imaginal space in which we meet again.

Soon after the first anniversary of Elizabeth's death, I dreamed:

> I'm in a car with my son. We see a group of children coming out of a house. One of them is Elizabeth at about age six. We stop the car and she gets in and sits on my lap facing me. I'm so glad to see her again that I start to cry. She doesn't say anything, but I see a kind of sadness and wisdom in her eyes. I realize that she knows she will not live a long life and I say to her, "You know, don't you?" Without words, she tells me, "Yes, I know." Then we sing together as we did when she was six. One of the songs is "When I'm on my journey, don't you weep after me." I feel intensely happy and sad at the same time. She seems very real, although I know she's no longer alive in her body.

Once again Elizabeth sits on my lap facing me, as she did in the dream of the rocking chair. But this time she is only six years old, as though she can now assume the bodily form of any given age. The look in her eyes, however, indicates a wisdom beyond her years. She seems to know that she will not have a long life, and to accept her fate. "When I'm on my journey, don't you weep after me" is a song that we often sang together when she was a child. It contains images of change, growth, and separation: "Every little river must flow out into the sea, ... Every little seedling must grow up to be a tree," and so on. The final line of each verse is "I don't want you to weep after me." In my first dream reunion with Elizabeth, she embraced me and told me to weep for her. Now, a year later, the waves of tears were abating and the "acceptance" stage of grief was appearing. Of course, I wept for her many times in the ensuing years. But if she was "on her journey," I did not want my tears to hold her back.

A few weeks later she made another dream appearance, this time as a three-year-old child who had come to live with me in my apartment in Zürich. I knew that the "real" Elizabeth had died, but I took the dream to mean that this playful, lively inner child had moved into the interior space of my psyche. I had been in training for almost three years and finally felt ready to read, study, and learn again. The dream suggested that my imaginal daughter would introduce a spirit of play and curiosity to my work. Knowing that Elizabeth was at home in my psyche as a playful three-year-old, a wise six-year-old, and an energetic and curious eighteen-year-old helped me bear the emptiness of life without her. Just as Judith Savage had observed, mourning was loosening my bond to the "real" Elizabeth and replacing it with a relationship to her inner image.

Notes

1 Cf. C. M. Parkes, *Bereavement: Studies of Grief in Adult Life*.
2 Homer, "Hymn to Demeter," 5.
3 For an account of Isis searching for Osiris and of the Gilgamesh epic, see G. Grubbs, *Bereavement Dreaming and the Individuating Soul*, 3–9.
4 *The Holy Bible*, King James Version, John 20:17 & 27, 1397–1398.
5 M.-L. von Franz, *On Dreams and Death*, 111–112.
6 *Ibid*, 112.
7 *Ibid.*
8 *Ibid.*
9 *Ibid.*, 114, italics in original.
10 *Ibid.*, xv.
11 H. Corbin, "*Mundus Imaginalis*," 9.
12 G. Mogenson, *Greeting the Angels*, 88, italics in original.
13 *Ibid.*
14 V. Kast, *A Time to Mourn*, 67–68.
15 C. M. Parkes, *Bereavement: Studies of Grief in Adult Life*, 64.
16 V. Kast, *A Time to Mourn*, 43.
17 Mogenson, *Greeting the Angels*, 89. The phrase "images that yet / Fresh images beget" is from W. B. Yeats's poem "Byzantium," in *The Collected Poems of W.B. Yeats* (New York: Macmillan, 1958), 243.
18 J. Keats, *Selected Poems and Letters*, 261.

19 Rilke, Letters to a Young Poet, 21.
20 M. Mahler, *The Psychological Birth of the Human Infant.*
21 J. Savage, *Mourning Unlived Lives*, 77.
22 G. Mogenson, *Greeting the Angels*, 32–33.
23 See Genesis 2:7: "And the Lord God formed man of the dust of the ground, and breathed into his nostrils the breath of life; and man became a living soul."
24 G. Mogenson, "The Afterlife of the Image," 97.

Chapter 6

The cure of souls

Coming home

Jung was twenty years old and a student at the University of Basel when his father, a Swiss Reform pastor, died in 1896. In *Memories*, he recalls that he stood by his father's deathbed and watched, fascinated, as the dying man drew his last breath. Soon he moved into his father's room and took on the role of the head of the household. Then, six weeks later, his father stood before him in a dream and announced that he had been on holiday, had recovered from his illness, and was on his way home. In the dream Jung wondered if his father would be annoyed with him for moving into his room, but Pastor Jung did not seem to mind. Nevertheless, confessed Jung, "I felt ashamed because I imagined that he was dead."[1] Two days later the dream was repeated, and again Jung reproached himself for thinking that his father had died.

This dream presents two contrasting viewpoints, that of the dream father and that of the dream ego. Jung's dream father thinks that he has recovered from his illness and is on his way home, but the dream ego, knowing that his father has died, is surprised to see him well and healthy again. In the dream Jung resolves the discrepancy by telling himself that he must have been mistaken about his father's death, but then he feels ashamed and reproaches himself for his false assumption. Upon awakening, however, he realizes anew that his father is dead and asks himself what it might mean that his father is still alive in his dreams. Jung's cognitive dissonance is understandable if we remind ourselves that his dreams, like my first dreams of Elizabeth and von Franz's dream of her dead father, occurred soon after his father's death. While our memories of the dead are fresh, vivid dream images make it seem that they are still alive in the outer world. Like Jung, we have trouble facing the truth that they are gone. The deceased can be dead in the external world and at the same time alive in the imaginal world, but it takes time for us to "get" this paradox. Slowly we must learn to differentiate between the world of objective reality and the imaginal world of dreams. Jung's task in the first weeks of bereavement was to accept the fact that his father was dead, while at the same time acknowledging the living presence of his father's image in his dreams. The two standpoints could co-exist without contradiction as long as he understood that they derived from two distinct levels of reality.

In view of Jung's complicated relationship with his father, his mixed reaction to his father's death is not surprising. Jung loved his father, sought his approval, and longed to share his profound experiences of God with him. But it appears that the elder Jung, a clergyman who had lost his faith, did not know how to relate to his precocious and inquisitive son. Jung's questions about religion were met with "the same old lifeless theological answers," and he soon realized that his father was "hopelessly entrapped by the Church."[2] When Pastor Jung died without resolving his inner conflict of faith or his outer conflict with his son, these problems were left for the son to address in his own life and work. Many of the father's concerns appear later in the son's dreams, as shall be seen in the following pages.

One possible interpretation of Jung's dream is that his father's unresolved theological questions were "coming home" to take up residence in his son's inner world. Reading Jung's account of his father's last months, it is clear that he was determined not to let himself be "entrapped" by the same fate that had befallen his father. If we interpret his dream subjectively, the image of his dead father might represent his own theological doubts, misgivings, and unanswered questions. Jung never implies that he wanted his father to die, but his account of his father's detrimental influence suggests that he knew that his inner "negative father" needed to die a symbolic death so that his own intellectual and spiritual life could flourish.

If we interpret Jung's dream objectively, new levels of meaning emerge. Jung was honest in stating that certain aspects of the father-son relationship were harmful to him and might have created further difficulties had his father lived. His mother seems to have understood this situation, because soon after her husband's death she remarked to her son, "He died in time for you."[3] Jung's comments on his mother's remark suggest that in her mind, his father had died in time to spare him any further psychological damage. If so, it is not surprising that he was troubled to find his father still alive in his dreams. But perhaps his dream father's announcement that he had recovered from his illness suggested the prospect of a more meaningful father-son relationship, in which the dream father could support rather than inhibit his son's psychological growth. In that case the recovered father figure would represent the possibility that Jung's negative father complex might eventually recover as well.

As mentioned above, soon after his father's death Jung moved into his room and took his place as the head of the household. Since his mother could not manage money, he had to take charge of the family finances and give her a weekly allowance. Thus the Oedipal relationship, in which the son "kills" his father and "marries" his mother, came perilously close to realization in Jung's life. I do not mean to suggest that Jung and his mother literally re-enacted the Oedipal drama. But at an early age Jung assumed his father's duties and began to serve as a surrogate husband to his mother. He appears to have had ambivalent feelings about being thrust into this position, as any young man would. He had to borrow money and find work in order to continue his studies, but this time of poverty taught him to value simple things. His new responsibilities brought a new sense of manliness and new freedom, he wrote.[4] It appears that once he recovered from the initial shock of his father's death, the world opened up for him and he pursued his scientific, intellectual, and religious interests with great energy. Summing up the meaning of his dreams of his father, Jung described them as "an unforgettable experience,... [which] forced me for the first time to think about life after death."[5]

Years later, Jung must have told his dreams of his father to Freud, for Freud discusses them in his paper "Formulations Regarding Two Principles in Mental Functioning," without revealing the dreamer's identity. In Freud's words, a young man "who had... looked after his father through a long and painful illness up to his death" repeatedly dreamed that "his father was again alive and he was talking to him as of old. But as he did so he felt it exceedingly painful that his father was nevertheless dead, only not aware of the fact."[6] As might be expected, Freud interpreted Jung's dream as a wish-fulfillment with an Oedipal twist. Assuming that Jung was ashamed that he had wanted his father to die, Freud viewed Jung's dreams as a compensation for his Oedipal guilt. In other words, Freud viewed the dream in terms of Jung's personal relationship to his father and not as a dream which "gives... importance to the psychology of the image."[7]

Commenting on Freud's interpretation, Greg Mogenson offers an alternative which would not minimize Jung's grief, overlook his conflicts with his father, or deny the possibility that the dream father might represent his personal father complex. An imaginal approach, suggests Mogenson, "would stick to the image itself" and follow it "through *its* transformations and changes."[8] Thus the dream figure of Jung's father might be viewed as an autonomous image inviting Jung to join him in a new inner relationship. According to this line of thought, Jung might have entered into an imaginal dialogue with his dream father, in which he could have come to "recognize himself... as the son of a subtle, psychological father, whom he ha[d] yet to get to know."[9] This possibility did not occur to Jung at the time of his father's death. But the seeds of future encounters with his dream father were planted in his initial dreams.

A dream consultation

Twenty-six years later, just before his mother's death in 1923, Jung had another dream in which his father appeared as though he was returning from a journey. He looked healthy and "had shed his air of paternal authoritarianism."[10] As in the earlier dream, he did not seem to realize that he was dead, but behaved as though he had been away and was now paying his son a visit. Jung wanted to ask him what he had been doing, show him his house, introduce him to his family, and tell him about his recent book on psychological types. But then he realized that his dream father had another agenda: he wanted to consult his son about marital psychology. But before Jung could answer his father's question, he woke up and the dream came to an abrupt end.[11]

At the time of this dream Jung was in his mid-forties. He had survived his break with Freud in 1912 and had established himself as an analyst, writer, and teacher in his own right. Married and the father of five children, he was also involved in a long-term extramarital relationship with Toni Wolff. A subjective analysis of his dream might have explored what his dream parents' troubled marriage represented in his own psyche. His dream father's concern with marital psychology might have hinted that it was time for Jung to examine the difficulties in his own marriage. But instead of approaching his dream subjectively, he viewed it objectively, as a dream visit from his dead father which portended his mother's imminent death. He did not venture an imaginal approach, which might have explored additional levels of meaning. His "confrontation with the unconscious" in 1912–1913 had convinced Jung of the autonomy of psychic images.[12] Therefore he might have noticed that his dream father had evolved into an autonomous figure who was busy tending to his own concerns in the afterlife. He had shed his paternal authority and now regarded his son as an expert in marital psychology. It would be interesting to know what might have happened if Jung had engaged in an imaginal exchange with his father following this dream, as he had done when he dropped into the unconscious and encountered various imaginal figures in 1913. He did not do so following this dream, but it does appear that his dream father was beginning to function as a mentor, guiding his son to undertake his study of marriage in his 1925 essay, "Marriage as a Psychological Relationship."

The cure of souls

Twenty years later, when Jung was in his sixties, his dead parents appeared in two dreams that hinted at work still to be done by their son. In these dreams it seems that Jung's dream father—and to some extent, his dream mother—have finally become the spiritual guides their son had wished for as a young man. In the first dream, Jung is exploring a large, unfamiliar wing of his house. He finds himself in a laboratory lined with shelves of bottles containing every sort of fish, and immediately realizes that it is his father's workroom.[13] Next to it is his mother's room, where she has set up "hanging pavilions" in which "ghostly married couples" can sleep. Jung's parents do not appear in the dream, but he senses their presence and knows that that they are working on the problem of the " 'cure of souls,' " which in fact was also his own task. He interprets the fish as a Christ symbol and the hanging beds as a humorous symbol of the *coniunctio* (the sacred marriage of the masculine and feminine principles). His parents' work on these matters indicated to him that his own work was still unfinished and "latent in the unconscious." But what might that unfinished work be? In 1951 Jung published *Aion* (*CW* 9ii), which included several sections on the symbol of the fish and an essay on the *Anima and Animus* (Jung's terms for the feminine and masculine principles). In 1955 (the year of his wife Emma's death) he published *Mysterium Coniunctionis* (*CW* 14), his study of the alchemical marriage of the masculine and feminine. At the time of his dream he must surely have been thinking about these matters, but his ideas had not yet assumed their final form. In other words, his dream alluded to subjects that were to keep him busy for many years to come.

Commenting on the dream, Jung states that he found it "remarkable" that his father was studying the fish, a Christ symbol. As a Christian Pastor, the elder Jung would have been responsible for the care of souls, which were represented in Christian art as "fish caught in Peter's net." But the fish in the laboratory are dead and preserved in bottles. How can the dream father hope to cure souls that are already dead? The answer, of course, is that he cannot. In Jung's view, his father's faith had been as dead as the bottled fish specimens. The pastor could not heal the wounds of others because his own wounds were unhealed. Later Jung compares his father to the fisher-king Amfortas in the Arthurian legends, whose wound would not heal because he himself had sinned. The tragedy of the elder Jung's life was that he had suffered like Christ without becoming aware that his own wound "was a consequence of the *imitatio Christi* [imitation of Christ]." And so the father's unfinished tasks were passed on to his son, and Jung continued the "cure of souls" by analyzing the symbol of the fish in *Aion* and the problem of suffering in *Answer to Job*.

So too with Jung's mother. Her unfinished work in the dream becomes a project that her son takes up later. In her case, the work has to do with ghostly married couples who are to sleep in the hanging pavilions she has set up for them. Jung describes the hanging beds as "uncanny"—the same word that he uses to describe his mother in *Memories*. As a child, Jung was sure that his mother had two personalities, "one innocuous and human, the other uncanny."[14] As an adolescent, he realized that his own personality also contained two elements, which he came to call his "No. 1" and "No. 2" personalities. No. 1 "was less intelligent, attentive, hard-working, decent, and clean than many other boys." In contrast, No. 2 was "mistrustful, remote from the world of men, but close to nature,... and above all close to the night, to dreams, and to whatever 'God' worked directly in him."[15] From this description, it appears that Jung identified with his mother's twofold personality, especially with the "archaic nature" of her "natural mind."[16] Thus it is possible that her uncompleted task, which Jung inherited, was to "marry" the two aspects of his personality into one cohesive whole. On the subjective level, therefore, the ghostly couples in the dream might represent the two sides of Jung's personality, which he sought to unite in the inner marriage that he came to call the *coniunctio*. The couples might also represent himself and his wife, suspended in an unusual sleeping arrangement that symbolized the state of their marriage. But since Jung did not explore this possibility, we can only guess as to its accuracy.

An objective view of the dream, on the other hand, might regard the ghostly couples as an image of Jung's parents' marriage. The hanging beds suggest that there was something ethereal in their relationship, an ungrounded element in their marital connection. In "real life," Jung's parents were not able to actualize the archetypal *coniunctio* in their relationship. Jung's marital triangle eventually achieved some stability only because all three of its members were willing to accept a compromise solution, unconventional though it was for their time. Thus the painful history of his parents' marriage, as well as the difficulties of his own, are suggested in the image of his parents living in an unexplored wing of his house and working in adjoining rooms. His parents' presence in his dream suggests that it was up to him to continue their work on the "cure of souls" by "marrying" the elements they were unable to unite. No wonder he believed that their dream images were directing him towards work that still remained to be done.

Custodian of the tombs

In a second dream from this period, Jung is visiting his father, who is living in a large country house and working as the custodian of the tombs of several famous people. To his son's great surprise, he has also become a distinguished biblical scholar, an achievement which he never attained in his lifetime.[17] In his study he opens a large Bible bound in fishskin and begins a swift and learned exegesis of an Old Testament passage, but his argument is so intelligent and complicated that Jung cannot follow it. Then the dream father leads his son up a narrow staircase to a large mandala-shaped room on the second floor, from the center of which another flight of stairs ascends to a spot high on the wall. At the top of the stairs is a small door, before which Jung's father says, "Now I will lead you into the highest presence." Then he kneels down and bows his head to the floor in a gesture of reverence. Jung imitates this gesture "with great emotion," but states that for some reason he cannot bring his forehead all the way to the floor. Before the dream ends, he suddenly knows that the door leads to the solitary chamber of Uriah, the general whom King David had betrayed "for the sake of his wife Bathsheba, by commanding his soldiers to abandon Uriah in the face of the enemy."

Once again Jung retrospectively interprets the images in this dream—the fishskin, the Old Testament passage, and the figure of Uriah—as a foreshadowing of the work he was to do in *Answer to Job*. In this interpretation the dream father represents his son's scholarly potential. Jung had been pursuing his interest in psychology, philosophy, and theology for decades, but his later work was still taking shape in his mind. On the imaginal level, the dream indicates that the figure of the father has evolved from a man recently recovered from an illness, to a student of ichthyology, to the custodian of the tombs of famous people and a learned biblical scholar. In earlier dreams he is either visiting his son or living in an unexplored wing of his son's house, but now he has found his own home and is busily involved in his own theological work. His personal history, marital problems, and spiritual struggles are not referenced in the dream, which focuses instead on his role as his son's teacher. Apparently his work on the "cure of souls" has finally come to fruition and he wants to share his new knowledge with his son.

A crucial point of distinction between Jung and his dream father remains, however, in their respective attitudes to the "highest presence." The dream father kneels and touches his forehead all the way to the floor, while the dream ego retains "some mental reservation" and leaves a millimeter to spare. In his analysis of this scene, Jung writes that although he ought to have touched his forehead all the way to the floor, something in him was "defiant and determined not to be a dumb fish." In his opinion his father had sacrificed his intellect to his religious faith, and had suffered greatly for it. Determined not to make the same mistake, Jung refuses to obey his dream father completely. Although the father has assumed a guiding role, the son still insists upon a degree of spiritual independence.

At the end of the dream Jung realizes that the "highest presence" refers to the chamber of Uriah, whose story is told in 2 Samuel 11. In the biblical story, King David seduces Uriah's wife Bathsheba, who becomes pregnant by him. In an attempt to make Uriah believe that he is the father of the child, David recalls him from the battlefield and tries to trick him into "lying with" his wife. When Uriah refuses, David arranges to have him assigned to the front lines of battle, where he is killed. After a suitable period of mourning, David marries Bathsheba and their son is born. But the Lord is displeased with David and the child becomes ill and dies. David repents of his sin, but he cannot erase its consequences.

Continuing his discussion of the dream, Jung interprets Uriah as a "prefiguration of Christ," a victim who was abandoned by God just as Uriah was abandoned by David. This association is somewhat perplexing, since Uriah was not exactly abandoned, but assigned to the front lines, where he perished at the hand of the enemy. Jung's interpretation of Uriah as a Christ-figure must have been justified in his mind, but it is not in keeping with the biblical text, in which Uriah's life (unlike Christ's) is sacrificed for a less than noble cause. Jung also viewed the allusion to Uriah as an indication that his wife would be "taken from [him] by death," when in fact it was Uriah, and not his wife, who died in the biblical story.

In conclusion, I find myself wondering why Jung interpreted his dream and the Old Testament story of Uriah this way. The answer may lie in another point of comparison, a personal analogy which Jung does not mention in *Memories*. David, Bathsheba, and Uriah were involved in a marital triangle, which was resolved by the death of one of its members. Jung also participated in a marital triangle by virtue of his relationship with Toni Wolff. In her biography of Jung, Deirdre Bair notes that both Fowler McCormick, a long-time friend of Carl and Emma Jung, and Joseph Henderson, an analyst who trained with Jung, concurred that "as much as was possible within a monogamous society, Jung had found a second wife in Toni and treated her with all the respect that such status implied."[18] At the time of Jung's dream Toni Wolff and Emma Jung were still living, but both women predeceased him by several years. And so it may be that years later, as he was writing *Memories*, he retrospectively regarded his dream of Uriah not only as a foreshadowing of his work on *Answer to Job*, but also of the ending of his own marital triangle with the death of his wife. It may be that in his eighties, while reviewing the dream of Uriah, Jung was reminded of the triangular relationship that had been so formative in his life, but he does not allude to this association. The fact that Uriah dwells in the chamber of the "highest presence" indicates the importance of the biblical story to Jung, but apparently he was unwilling to discuss it further in the public forum of his memoirs.

In Jung's dreams of his dead parents, the parental images change with the passage of time. Six weeks after his death, Jung's father comes to life again in

Jung's inner world as a recovered version of his former self, causing a good deal of confusion for his son. This early recurring dream stresses Jung's grief reaction as he struggles to detach himself from his memories of his living father and absorb the truth that his father is really dead. In Jung's middle years, the image of his dream father has evolved from a paternal authority figure to a man who recognizes his son's authority and seeks his advice on the subject of marriage. By implication, Jung's "uncanny" mother has been waiting for his father in the afterlife and is preparing to resume their troubled relationship. By the time Jung was in his mid-sixties, his dream parents are engaged in their own work. His dream father has become an expert on theology and Jung's dream ego struggles to understand what he is saying. It is important to remember that in *Memories*, Jung was viewing his dreams of his dead parents in a rear-view mirror, so to speak, with the intention of showing that their appearance foreshadowed his future work. He did not choose to examine the parental figures in association to his own personal issues, or as autonomous images which continued to evolve in his psyche. Perhaps he thought about these matters in private but decided not to include his ideas in his memoirs, just as he did not include other personal information. Nevertheless it is clear that Jung's parents did leave him with a legacy of unfinished business to pursue in his own work. In death they became what they could not be in life: their son's spiritual mentors and guides.

Notes

1 C. G. Jung, *Memories*, 117.
2 *Ibid.*, 113.
3 *Ibid.*, 116.
4 *Ibid.*
5 *Ibid.*, 117.
6 S. Freud, "Formulations Regarding the Two Principles in Mental Functioning," 20.
7 G. Mogenson, "The Afterlife of the Image," 93.
8 *Ibid.*, 96, emphasis in original.
9 *Ibid.*, 95–96.
10 C. G. Jung, *Memories*, 346. This dream was also discussed in Chapter 3.
11 *Ibid.*, 347.
12 For an account of this experience and its influence on Jung, see *Memories*, Chapter VI, 194–225, and *The Red Book*.
13 Jung's account of this dream is found in *Memories*, 239–242.
14 *Ibid.*, 66.
15 *Ibid.*, 61–62.
16 *Ibid.*, 68.
17 Jung's account of this dream is found in *Memories*, 244–247.
18 D. Bair, *Jung: A Biography*, 560.

Chapter 7

The wound that heals

The light of truth

In the Homeric "Hymn to Demeter," the goddess is unable to rest until she discovers what has happened to her daughter. Her flaming torches and the bright beams of the Sun symbolize the light of truth: even if the knowledge burns, she is ready to face reality. The need to know the truth is a natural development in the process of mourning. As numbness dissipates, the bereaved often feel compelled to review the events leading up to their loved one's passing. They question doctors, comb through medical records, visit the place of death, and replay the final moments of their beloved's life over and over in their minds. For example, Joan Didion wrote that she repeatedly reviewed in her mind the events preceding her husband's fatal heart attack, as if to alter the outcome or at least make sense of it. But in her confusion she gave the wrong address to the hospital holding his medical records, and did not receive a copy of his autopsy report until almost a year after his death. Finally she realized that there was nothing she could have done to prevent the inevitable. "Only after I read the autopsy report did I stop trying to reconstruct the collision, the collapse of the dead star. The collapse had been there all along, invisible, unsuspected," she wrote.[1] As her "year of magical thinking" came to an end, Didion finally accepted that her husband was not coming back. Truth broke through her wall of denial, but then she faced the prospect of life without him. "The craziness is receding but no clarity is taking its place," she wrote. "I look for resolution and find none."[2]

Reliving the trauma

How *does* resolution come about? How does clarity come to those who mourn? To understand this process, it helps to know how trauma affects the body and psyche. Traumatic events take many forms: experiencing physical or sexual abuse, participating in and surviving war, witnessing a catastrophic event, or losing a loved one to violence, to name just a few. In response to these painful experiences our mental "fabric" begins to unravel. The ego, the central organizing structure of consciousness, can no longer "keep it together." Expressions such as *falling apart*, *falling to pieces*, and *coming unglued* reflect this disjointed state, in which memories, thoughts, feelings, and physical sensations occur at random, with no apparent connection to outer events. Irish poet W. B. Yeats phrased it dramatically in "The Second Coming" when he wrote, "Things fall apart; the centre cannot hold; Mere anarchy is loosed upon the world."[3] In response to severe trauma the ego may dissociate, so that the person has the sensation of observing events from the outside, like a spectator at a play. Or the memory of an event may be repressed altogether, until dreams or another person's reminder bring it back to consciousness. Splitting, depersonalization, and repression are powerful defenses, but as Donald Kalsched points out in *The Inner World of Trauma*, they may have a constructive function as well.[4] Suffering the full impact of a major trauma all at once can be mentally and emotionally unbearable. Severing the connection between consciousness, sensation, thinking, feeling, and memory is the psyche's way of protecting itself against the possible development of serious psychological disorders such as major depression, mania, or psychosis.

Healing from trauma involves the slow gathering, naming, and piecing together of the scattered shards of psychic experience. Cognition, emotion, sensation, and memory must be reconnected and reforged into a coherent whole. This painful and painstaking process happens at its own pace and cannot be rushed. For example, Joan Didion's repeated reconstruction of the events preceding her husband's heart attack helped her arrive at a cognitive understanding of what had happened to him. Repeatedly reading his autopsy report convinced her that she could not have prevented his death. Being swept repeatedly into emotional vortexes (despite her best efforts to avoid them) made it possible for her to feel her sadness, anger, helplessness, and anxiety in limited doses, rather than all at once. Traveling to California to be with her critically ill daughter stirred up memories of happier times and helped her fold them into the hard reality of the present.[5] As she observed in hindsight, this was the process by which grief was gradually transformed into mourning. "Until now I had been able only to grieve, not mourn," she wrote. "Grief was passive. Grief happened. Mourning, the act of dealing with grief, required attention."[6] When the ego is able to take an active role in the task of psychic reconstruction, the healing work of mourning can begin. But as Peter Levine observes in *Waking the Tiger: Healing Trauma*, the mental and emotional reenactment of trauma is risky business.[7] Instead of fostering healing, reliving an event may actually re-traumatize the survivor and become an obstacle to recovery. Memories and flashbacks can activate the same state of heightened emotional and physical arousal that occurred at the time of the original event. Like the proverbial deer in the headlights, we may freeze rather than mobilize ourselves to confront or flee from the traumatic stimulus. In order to alleviate this state of acute arousal, it is necessary to discharge the physical and emotional energy built up when body and mind freeze in an attempt to avoid pain. According to Bessel van der Kolk, another expert on trauma, practices such as EMDR,[8] yoga, and Tai Chi enable survivors to process traumatic memories and affects gradually.[9] Physical movement can "thaw" the body and brain, thereby activating healing energy. In the Homeric "Hymn to Demeter," the goddess spends a long time wandering through cities and fields after she learns her daughter's fate. She seems to know instinctively that physical activity is exactly what she needs. When she meets the daughters of the king, she takes action to move beyond her traumatized state by greeting the young women, asking them to help her find work, and becoming the nursemaid to their baby brother. This course of action does not mitigate her sorrow, but it does set the process of healing in motion. In similar fashion, Joan Didion finally began to sort through her husband's papers, go for long walks, and write about her grief. Once she began, the words poured out of her. For the bereaved, such activities mark a shift from passive suffering to active mourning, from disintegration to reintegration and healing.

Laura's story

In the weeks immediately following Elizabeth's death I could not bear to know the details of the accident and did not want to hear more than the basic facts of the story. But as time passed, questions began to rise to the surface of my mind. Why had Elizabeth and her friends been walking down the side of a major highway in the middle of the night? How did the drunk driver happen to come by at just that moment? Did he see them? Why didn't he stop? Did he know what he had done? How did it happen that Michael and Elizabeth were hit by his car, while Laura was not? Finally I realized that I was ready to hear the truth—but I needed help from someone who had been there. Laura, still in grief herself, came to visit and we sat on my living-room sofa and had a long talk. By then she was ready to tell her story and I was ready to hear it. I also wanted to reassure her that I was glad she was alive, because I suspected that as the only survivor of the accident, she might be dealing with a good deal of guilt. Our conversation answered many of my questions and addressed her need to talk about her trauma. In retrospect, I think that our talk helped both of us move into active mourning, the act of dealing with grief.

As Laura spoke, I learned that the three friends, on a last-minute weekend jaunt, had run out of gas in the middle of the night. Elizabeth, who was driving while Michael rested, apparently did not notice that the car's gas gauge had fallen to "empty." At first the three young people tried to flag down passing cars, but no one stopped. Finally they decided to go for help and found two Highway Department workers who promised to bring them some gas. Walking back to their car, they entered an access ramp and continued three abreast along the right side of the highway, Laura on the left, Michael in the middle, and Elizabeth on the right. They thought they were on the shoulder, but in fact they were in the far right-hand lane, walking in the direction of traffic. The night was dark and the highway was dimly lit. Laura recalled that they were happy to have found help and were singing as they marched along. Suddenly, she heard a car coming up behind them at high speed. She could not remember if its headlights were on or not. Then she felt a rush of air as the car sped by. When she turned to the right to see what had happened, her friends had disappeared. Many yards ahead, the car's tail lights flashed as the driver braked briefly and then drove on. Then she saw Elizabeth lying near the guardrail on the right side of the road and Michael lying in the middle of the highway to the left. She ran to her friends, covered Elizabeth up, directed an approaching car away from Michael's body, and ran around picking up shoes and other items that had been scattered in the collision, as though trying to restore order to the chaotic scene. Finally the police arrived and took her to the hospital, where she was found to have sustained no physical injuries. But that morning she had to identify the bodies of her friends, help the police locate their families, and call her parents to come and take her home. In the months and years that followed, she testified at several hearings and finally at the trial of the driver (who had eventually turned himself in to the police). I know that each time she told her story, her own wounds reopened. But by holding up the torch of truth and facing the reality of what had happened to her, this courageous young woman took an active role in her own healing. Our common loss made us companions in grief and brought us closer to Elizabeth and to each other. I will always be grateful to her, for by telling her story she helped me heal as well.

In the coming months the story continued to unfold. As I talked to Michael's parents, police investigators, and attorneys, more details emerged. Gradually the circumstances of that night, which at first had seemed like a random scattering of unrelated incidents, began to fit together into a more coherent whole. Each conversation helped me integrate a bit more of the truth and make some sense of the sequence of events. I also learned that many people—even those who had never met Elizabeth—were touched by her death, and that I was not alone in my grief. Eventually I visited the scene of the accident, met lawyers and police officers, gave my own deposition, attended several hearings, and wrote a "victim impact statement" for the court record. Elizabeth's father and brother and Michael's family wrote statements as well. Finally, her father and I attended the trial of the young man whose irresponsible decisions had ended our daughter's life. I dreaded the encounter with him, but I needed to see him face to face. I also wanted him to see us so that he could not deny the reality of what he had done. Because of him two gifted young people were dead, a third was deeply traumatized, and the lives of three families were in tatters. I wanted him to see the human impact of his actions and never forget it.

At the trial, he was convicted of driving while impaired and of leaving the scene of the accident. He spent a brief time in prison and his driver's license was revoked for ten years. Much later, a financial settlement was reached in the civil suit. It was a great relief when the legal proceedings were finally over, but nothing could alter the reality that Elizabeth and Michael were dead. We knew the truth about the accident—or as much of it as we could piece together—but the prospect of life without them stretched before us like a blighted landscape. As one of Elizabeth's friends, himself an attorney, said to me after her funeral, "Susan, we were robbed." Elizabeth and Michael were robbed of their lives, those who loved them were robbed of the joy of watching their promise unfold, and Laura was robbed of her peace of mind and the companionship of her two best friends. Many people were wounded, including the young man who made the fatal mistake of driving while impaired and the friends who did not insist on taking away his car keys. We will all bear the scars for the rest of our days.

Knowing the truth is only the first step in the process of what Laura wryly called "coming to terms." The word "closure" has become a catchphrase for the notion of a neat and tidy resolution of emotional and psychological trauma. But anyone who has ever lost someone—and no human being is exempt from that experience—knows that a neat and tidy resolution to grief is impossible. It is inhuman to suggest that the bereaved can and should "get over" the loss of a loved one quickly and easily. In the Homeric Hymn, Demeter refused to "get over it" when she would not listen to the Sun, who tried to persuade her that Hades was not such a bad match for her daughter after all. Her "mother grief" was still intense and she had not yet begun to heal.[10]

Dreams that wound and heal

Cognitive awareness of the circumstances of a traumatic event is one thing; emotional healing is quite another. As the fragments of the psyche slowly knit back together, reunion dreams provide a measure of solace. But darker dreams are also integral to the process. For example, on the night after her fiancé George's death, Elena dreamed:

> I embrace George, I feel very close to him and am overcome by feelings of tenderness. Suddenly I feel him become colder and colder. He dies in my arms. I am filled with despair. I know that nothing can bring him back again, that I can no longer embrace him, no longer feel him.[11]

Verena Kast notes that this dream held paradoxical meaning for Elena. At first the sense of George's presence was "wonderful," but as he grew cold and died in her arms, the dream emphasized the reality of his death and prepared her to accept his physical absence. This dream wounded in order to heal. Elena's grief wound had to be opened, cleansed, and stitched back together so that no infection remained and deep healing could occur.

In the months following Elizabeth's death I had many dreams in which I visited the site of the accident (although I had not seen it yet), tended to her injuries, and slowly came to accept the fact that she was dead. Those wounding and healing dreams helped me experience and integrate the reality of her death, almost as though I had been there when it happened. The first dream occurred about two months after the accident:

Elizabeth, Laura and I go back to the scene of the accident. We are riding bicycles and the two girls are slightly ahead of me. Elizabeth is riding with "no hands" and combing her hair with her fingers as she rides. I think, "No wonder she got killed!" and feel angry at her for being careless. But at the same time I know that she is dead and that nothing can hurt her now.

We ride down the empty entrance ramp onto the highway. On the right side, repairs have been made and a guardrail installed. It is broad daylight, not the middle of the night. I catch up to the girls and ask them, "Is this the place?" They say that it is. I say, "I thought so" and feel very strange.

Then I ask Elizabeth if she knew anything at the time of impact. She says, "I heard 'Mrs. X' say, 'This is the get-off place.'" Laura says that she saw Elizabeth fall backwards and heard her make a sound.

Then Elizabeth and I are in the back of an ambulance. I am holding her and caressing her head, feeling horrified and trying to comfort her. She is smiling her little smile and looking just as she did as a child when I gave her head rubs. I pay special attention to her head because that was the site of her fatal injury.

At the time of this dream I was just starting to wonder about the events preceding the accident. When I visited the scene several months later, I was amazed to discover that the dream had presented an uncannily accurate picture of it. The entrance ramp, the highway, the guardrail—the setting was just as I had dreamed it. Perhaps the dream was hinting that it was time for me to bring the light of truth to bear on the facts of the matter. But the dream's deeper emphasis was upon the dream ego's emotional reaction to the situation. Beginning with anger at Elizabeth and ending with concern about her head injury, the dream sorted the emotional tangle of grief into its many component threads. Anxiety, anger, resignation, sadness, curiosity, tenderness: all were part of the jumbled mix. By identifying them as discrete elements, the dream helped me name and accept them without judgment. Like a mirror, it reflected the affective experience of grief back to me so that I could begin to put my psychic experience into words.

Dreams often follow a dramatic structure and unfold like the action in a play. The first section of the dream sets the stage and defines the setting. Then the characters are introduced and the dream's action begins. This dream places special emphasis on the dream ego's affective response to each event. Once an emotion has been experienced and identified, the action of the dream moves on to the next scene. As the dream opens, the girls and I are riding bicycles, a form of transportation that Elizabeth used often in high school and college. She and Laura ride ahead of me, like guides leading me to an unfamiliar place. But just as the "real" Elizabeth let the car run out of gas and walked down the middle of an entrance ramp, the dream Elizabeth seems oblivious to danger, riding her bike with no hands and combing her hair with her fingers. I react, as I did in my premonitory dream of the horses, with anxiety about her safety. But then I feel angry, and with the anger comes the unwelcome thought that her carelessness may have contributed to the accident. From the medical report I had been relieved to learn that no drugs or alcohol had been involved (although I had no reason to think that they would be). And yet it was undeniable that the three young people had not been paying close attention to the gas gauge and that Elizabeth, as the driver, was at least partially responsible for the lapse. Even in the dream, it was painful to admit that I was angry. But as I realized that she was now beyond further harm, my mood changed from anger to resignation.

The image of hair is prominent in this dream, as it was in several others. In actual life, Elizabeth wore her hair simply and paid little attention to styling it. But in the dream she is combing it with her fingers as she rides along. As a dream symbol, hair often represents the ideas and thoughts that grow from the head. Elizabeth's attempt to separate and tame the tangled strands of her thinking certainly reflected my own attempt to untangle and comb through the many elements of my response to her death. Her dream behavior reflected my own, although her carefree attitude did not mirror my confusion and distress.

In the second part of the dream, the girls and I approach the scene of the accident. In actual life it occurred at about 4:00 a.m., but in the dream we are in broad daylight, implying that the light of consciousness is shining on the inner "scene." Realizing that the girls know more than I do, I ask them two questions. The first, "Is this the place?" has to do with the exact location of Elizabeth's death. In the waking world it was an ordinary spot near a guardrail on the side of a major highway. But catastrophic events have the power to transform ordinary spots into sacred ground. In my psyche, the site had come to represent the *thin place* through which Elizabeth had passed into the next world. When the girls say that we have reached the spot, I feel "very strange," as though I am standing on the threshold of eternity. If Demeter had stood at the spot where Persephone vanished into the underworld, she might have felt the same thing. (Since Elizabeth's death I have become more aware of the many roadside memorials marking spots where people have lost their lives in auto accidents. Crosses, flowers, and stuffed animals are placed there as tributes to those who have died. Michael's mother told me later that she had placed two red carnations at the spot where our children were killed. I was deeply grateful and wished that I had been able to be with her.)

My second question in the dream has to do with what Elizabeth knew and felt at the moment of impact. The medical report said that she had died instantly, but I could not help wondering if she knew what was happening to her. I fervently hoped that she had not suffered, but at the same time I did not want to think that she had died without a moment to prepare. In the dream, her response to my question is unexpected. All she says is, "I heard Mrs. X say, 'This is the get-off place.'" Her answer made no sense to me at the time. Mrs. X, a woman I knew slightly, had also lost a child—but there the thread of association ended. Years later, however, Marie-Louise von Franz's book *On Dreams and Death* shed light on the figure of Mrs. X. Von Franz describes "the Greek portrayal of death as a bird-shaped female being (with a human upper body), the frightful *keres*, who carried the souls of the dead away to Hades."[12] The image of the *keres* was striking to me because Mrs. X's name included an allusion to birds. I do not mean to identify Mrs. X herself with the *keres* figure, but her name points to "those fateful personal death demons that carried away the dying person."[13] I think of the *keres* figure now as an example of psyche's uncanny ability to "choose" just the right archetypal symbol to convey the power of an outer event. Just as a bird of prey swoops down and seizes a mouse in its talons, sudden death strikes without warning and carries unsuspecting individuals into the next world.

Returning to the dream, the next words come from Laura, who says that she saw Elizabeth fall backwards and heard her make a sound. I did not ask Laura if this had been her actual experience, but it may well have been. The dream stresses her important role as a witness who could verify the sequence of events in the dream world, just as she had done in the outer world by telling me her story and testifying at the trial. The final scene of the dream focuses again on the dream ego's emotional response to the accident. Elizabeth and I are in the back of an ambulance and I am holding her and tending to her head wound. She is still alive, although seriously hurt. This scene reflects my wish that I could have held and comforted her at the moment of death. Perhaps it is even a compensation for the fact that I was unable to do so in actual life. Jung addresses this need in his commentary on *The Tibetan Book of the Dead* when he writes,

> Th[e] cult of the dead is rationally based on the belief in the supra-temporality of the soul, but its irrational basis is to be found in the psychological need of the living to do something for the departed. This is an elementary need which forces itself upon even the most "enlightened" individuals when faced by the deaths of relatives and friends. That is why, enlightenment or no enlightenment, we still have all manner of ceremonies for the dead.[14]

For me, holding Elizabeth and caressing her head in the dream satisfied that "elementary need." As the site of her fatal injury, her head required special attention. But as a dream symbol, it invited an archetypal interpretation as well. According to Edward Edinger, the image of the dead head, or *caput mortuum*, is associated with the initial phase of the alchemical process.[15] (Jung regarded alchemy, the process that sought to transform lead or other base metals into gold, as a symbolic representation of individuation, the quest for psychological wholeness.) The first phase has to do with the beginning or "head" of the work, in which darker, or "shadow," contents of the unconscious often manifest as painful emotions and disturbing thoughts. By tending to Elizabeth's wounded head, the dream ego attends to this dark material, suggesting that the psyche may now be ready to handle the painful emotions and thoughts associated with acute grief. The dream ends with the hint that "paying special attention to her head" will be an ongoing task of mourning.

In the following months I had several more dreams of visiting the site of the accident. In one dream, a car went off the road and into a ditch. A young female passenger fell into the water and drowned, and I felt horrified as I watched her body start to disintegrate. There were also two dreams in which the accident vehicle was a horse-drawn wagon, like the chariot of Hades in the myth of Demeter and Persephone. In one of these dreams I was searching for the exact location of the accident so that I could find and bury Elizabeth's body. These dreams included images of rotting and putrefaction, corresponding to the alchemical process of *mortificatio*, in which shadow material is reduced to its basic components. Burying the "body" of painful thoughts and affects in the earth reminded me of the dream in which Elizabeth said, "Let your tears fertilize my ground." Perhaps that dark "body" represented the seed that had to die so that new growth could emerge from the ground of the psyche.

Other dreams from this period repeated the image of the wounded head and the tending of injuries. In them, Elizabeth was alive again and seemed to be on the mend. In one dream she was wearing a plaster cast on her head, and in two others she had completely recovered. In response, I felt skeptical and thought, "But she had a skull fracture!" In another dream I took her to the doctor for a post-accident checkup. When I asked her if she had any symptoms, she replied, "Only a headache now and then." Then she declared in a defiant tone, "But I *am* going to the beach this weekend!" Considering the extent of her injuries, I could scarcely believe that she was doing so well. From one point of view, these dreams reinforced the denial of death and maintained the fiction of a miraculous recovery. But even as I dreamed, I knew that Elizabeth was no longer alive on the physical plane. The healing was taking place on the psychological level as she became a living image in my inner world.

Later I discussed my dreams with Emmanuel Kennedy, author of "The Alchemy of Death."[16] In his view, dreams of healing indicate that the dead are undergoing a process of recovery and transformation in the "hereafter." When we dream that they are hurt, visiting a doctor, or recovering from their injuries, we can assume that they are engaged in their own work of healing, he suggested. If we dream that they are whole again, we can infer that the healing process is complete. At this time, Elizabeth's dream image was undergoing a profound transformation. My dreams contained elements of both of Mogenson's types of bereavement dreams, including my personal grief but also attending to Elizabeth's ongoing imaginal life in my psyche. Her defiant remark about going to the beach suggested that the imaginal Elizabeth was determined to live an autonomous life, even though I might object. In spite of my tears I had to laugh, because it was so like her to insist upon doing things her own way. It was good to know that even in the dream world, she was very much herself.

"I could have died!"

A final dream from this period suggests that the living and the dead can assist each other in their transition to a new relationship:

> Elizabeth is telling me what happened on the night she died. She says that the "aura" or spiritual protective shield that surrounds each person was withdrawn for a few seconds, as though her guardian angel had relaxed his guard for a moment. Then she seems to understand how serious his lapse was and exclaims, "I could have died!" I start to cry, take her face in my hands, look her right in the eye and say to her, "Honey, you did die." I realize that she still isn't completely aware of what happened to her and that she needs reality testing from me, just as I need it from her.

As the dream begins, Elizabeth is speaking about the circumstances of her death—this time from a spiritual perspective. What she says about "auras" and her guardian angel is fascinating, but even in the dream I felt somewhat skeptical about it. Elizabeth, however, seems to be convinced that her guardian angel had something to do with the accident. She does not blame him for relaxing his guard, but states matter-of-factly that this is what happened. Until this dream, I had never given much thought to the existence of guardian angels. But my analyst, a Roman Catholic, had been brought up to believe in them. Since I respected him deeply, I began to consider the idea, but I was troubled by the possibility that Elizabeth's angel had relaxed his guard for a minute. Are guardian angels fallible? Do they make mistakes? Fall down on the job? Leave us in the lurch, just when we need them the most? In my dream, Elizabeth seemed to imply that angels, like humans, have free will, make choices, and even let their attention wander at times. In other words, angels are imperfect beings, capable of misjudgment and error. Everyone knows what it feels like to experience a close call—an accident that was avoided at the last minute, a disaster that almost happened, but didn't. Elizabeth was suggesting that these near misses come about when guardian angels lower their guard, then raise it again, just in time. Perhaps there are situations (such as war, natural disaster, murder, and genocide) in which environmental factors and malicious intent overwhelm even the most vigilant guardian angel. Or perhaps, when it is time for us to die, our guardian angels gently withdraw the "aura" that has protected us throughout our lives. Of course, these questions are pure speculation. In the end, the image of a guardian angel withdrawing his guard lends the circumstances of the accident a spiritual significance and emphasizes that we mere mortals are not in absolute control of our fate.

After Elizabeth's comments about her guardian angel, the tone of the dream changes abruptly. Suddenly she grasps the import of what she has just said and exclaims, "I could have died!" Now she seems to regard the accident as a close call, a near-disaster that was averted just in time. Or perhaps she is under the impression that she was injured, but did not die. This interpretation is in keeping with the earlier dream in which she is being rushed to the hospital in an ambulance. All at once I realize that she does not know she is dead and that it is up to me to tell her. I do this as gently as I can, taking her face in my hands, looking her in the eye, and calling her "honey." But still the moment is painful, because in saying the words to her, I am also saying them to myself.

The notion that the dead need our help in coming to terms with their fate was new to me. It reminded me of Jung's commentary on *The Tibetan Book of the Dead*, in which he notes the need of the living to do something for the departed. But another association came to mind as well. A year before her death, Elizabeth had given me a copy of that ancient Buddhist text as a Christmas present. She knew that I was interested in Jung and that he had written a commentary on it—but even so, it seemed unusual for a seventeen-year-old girl to give that particular book to her mother. I did not read it right away, but later I learned that it includes instructions to be read to dying (or recently deceased) persons to guide them through the *Bardo*, the realm between death and reincarnation into their next life. The text is designed to help the deceased realize that they have died, recognize the peaceful and wrathful spirits they will encounter in the *Bardo*, and (if possible) avoid being reborn into the endless cycle of death and rebirth. I do not know how Elizabeth had learned about the book, but I knew that the notion of reincarnation had fascinated her. Now I wondered, "What if she is stuck in the *Bardo*, unable to find her way out because she does not realize that she has died? What if *I* am stuck in an emotional *Bardo* of my own because I have not fully accepted her death? And what if unconsciously she had given me this book to help both of us deal with what was about to happen?"

Of course, I had no way of knowing whether Elizabeth was *literally* stuck in the *Bardo* and needed my help to move beyond it. But I did know that I was stuck in my own *Bardo*, cognitively aware of her death but still trying to accept it emotionally. On the subjective level, that was the meaning of the "guardian angel" dream: in telling Elizabeth "You *did* die," I was telling *myself* the same thing, freeing her dream image to live its autonomous life, and freeing myself to move beyond "the wallowing grief of the sentimental mourner."[17] Perhaps I was beginning to understand that her departure from the physical world might be a prelude to new life in the imaginal world. A year after her death, I was gradually learning that my dreams possessed a wisdom of their own. They were guiding me along the precarious path of mourning, and I hoped that they would continue to show me the way.

Notes

1   J. Didion, *The Year of Magical Thinking*, 207.
2   *Ibid.*, 225.
3   W. B. Yeats, "The Second Coming," in *The Collected Poems of W. B. Yeats*, 184.
4   Donald Kalsched, *The Inner World of Trauma: Archetypal Defenses of the Personal Spirit*.
5   Quintana Roo Dunne died in 2005. Didion's book *Blue Nights* is her tribute to her daughter.
6   J. Didion, *The Year of Magical Thinking*, 143.

7 For a full exposition of the activation and thawing of the "freeze" response, see P. A. Levine, *Waking the Tiger: Healing Trauma*.
8 Eye movement desensitization and reprocessing.
9 B. A. van der Kolk, A. C. McFarlane, and L. Weisaeth, eds., *Traumatic Stress*.
10 C. Mathes coined the term "mother grief" in her book *And a Sword Shall Pierce your Heart*.
11 J. Didion, *The Year of Magical Thinking*, 207.
12 M.-L. von Franz, *On Dreams and Death*, 51.
13 *Ibid.*, 60.
14 C. G. Jung, "Psychological Commentary," in *The Tibetan Book of the Dead*, 1.
15 E. F. Edinger, *Anatomy of the Psyche: Alchemical Symbolism in Psychotherapy*, 165.
16 Personal conversation with Emmanuel X. Kennedy, author of "The Alchemy of Death."
17 G. Mogenson, "The Afterlife of the Image," 97.

Chapter 8

"Remember me!"

The child in the fire

The desire to memorialize a loved one after death is an instinctive response to loss. As noted in the previous chapter, it meets "the psychological need of the living to do something for the departed," and it explains the origin of "all manner of ceremonies for the dead."[1] The instinct reflects the desire to find, produce, or create something to take the place of the one we have lost. In the myth of Demeter, this energy manifests when the goddess agrees to become the nurse of the king's infant son, Demophoon. Seeking to make him "free of age and death," she anoints him with ambrosia, breathes on him, and places him each night in the hearth fire in an attempt to burn away his mortality.[2] Soon he begins to resemble a god himself—until his mother grows suspicious, sees her son burning in the fire, and flies into a panic. Then Demeter snatches the child from the flames, reveals herself as a goddess, and berates the child's mother for being so foolish. She initiates a festival to honor Demophoon and orders the king to build her a shrine, but when it is completed she sits down and pines for her lost daughter once again. Her attempt to immortalize a human child has failed, and even the beautiful shrine cannot fill the emptiness in her heart.

I interpret Demeter's efforts to immortalize the king's son as an attempt to create a surrogate child to replace her lost daughter. When that endeavor fails, she hopes that the sumptuous shrine will satisfy her yearning. It is as though she is attempting to find a transitional object to alleviate what Winnicott calls "anxiety of depressive type."[3] In mourning, we search for such objects in our immediate environment, but we also create them in order to mitigate the pain of loss. We may hope that a new love, another child, or a challenging project will fill our inner emptiness. These efforts, like Demeter's, are apt to disappoint, because what we seek cannot be found outside ourselves. But at least our life energy is flowing again and seeking a creative outlet.

Planning a funeral or memorial service is often our first attempt to create a tribute to the departed. The task becomes even more meaningful if our loved ones have expressed their wishes regarding their last rites. At times even the young and healthy make their desires known. As I mentioned in Chapter 1, Elizabeth had said that "if anything ever happened" to her, she wanted her body to be cremated and she did not want green Astroturf covering the ground at her gravesite. I do not know why she thought of these things, but being aware of her wishes made the painful task of planning her funeral a little less difficult. It was also natural to establish a memorial fund at her school to support the Russian-American exchange program in which she had participated. Doing this honored her and contributed to an activity that would benefit other young people as well.

Like all rituals, funeral rites mark the end of one phase of life and herald the beginning of another. By treating the bodies of the dead with respect, creating a safe container for the emotions of grief, and strengthening the bonds between survivors, funerals perform an invaluable emotional and psychological function. They help the bereaved begin to move from a corporal relationship with the deceased to an imaginal, spiritual one. They also affirm our connection to the "higher powers," however we may define them. The following section examines funeral rites as depicted in Homer's epics *The Iliad* and *The Odyssey*.

Rites of burning: Homer

The ancient Greeks believed that if proper funeral rites were not observed, the "higher powers" (the gods) would grow angry and punish survivors with natural disasters, illness, or even death. They also believed that deprived of the proper ceremonies, the dead would not be allowed to enter the underworld and take their rightful place among the shades. Homer's two great epics, *The Iliad* and *The Odyssey*, contain several episodes in which the spirits of the dead plead with the living to perform their rites of passage. Although these stories originated almost 3,000 years ago, their insights into bereavement and mourning are still relevant today. Jung often observed that the gods of old appear today in the form of psychological symptoms and complexes. In clinical terms, the "gods" can reveal themselves in the psychotic depression, debilitating anxiety, and delusional thinking associated with pathological grief. Mythological and psychological language point to the same fundamental truth: meaningful funeral rites honor the dead and enable survivors to contain and express the powerful affects that might otherwise overwhelm them.

The Iliad, which recounts the story of the Trojan War, includes an episode in which a fallen warrior requests his proper funeral honors. After being slain by the Trojan hero Hector, the ghost of Patroclus appears to his friend Achilles in a dream and begs him to perform the rites:

> Never was I uncared for
> in life, but am in death. Accord me burial
> in all haste: Let me pass the gates of Death.
> Shades that are images of used-up men
> motion me away, will not receive me

among their hosts beyond the river. I wander
about the wide gates and the hall of Death.
Give me your hand. I sorrow.
When thou shalt have allotted me my fire
I will not fare here from the dark again.[4]

Still in the dream, Achilles attempts to embrace Patroclus, but his friend's shade retreats into the earth like smoke. When he wakes up, Achilles cuts off his hair to honor his friend and erects a magnificent funeral pyre, upon which he sacrifices Patroclus's dogs and horses as well as droves of other animals and twelve Trojan captives. When the flames finally die down, he goes to his rest knowing that he has aided his friend's passage into the realm of the dead. The ritual, however, is tinged with pathos, for the dream also includes a prophecy in which Patroclus foretells the death of Achilles and asks that their bones be buried together in one urn. In response, Achilles instructs his men to gather his friend's bones and lay them in the golden urn to await the day of his own death. The next day he plans an elaborate array of funeral games, but when the celebration is over, he lies awake and continues to weep. Then he defiles Hector's corpse by dragging it around the tomb of Patroclus and refusing to release it to the Trojans. The funeral rites may have helped Patroclus cross into Hades, but they have not helped Achilles move beyond his grief. He is tied (literally) to the body of Hector and the physical level of loss—and because he is mired in grief, the war between the Greeks and Trojans comes to a standstill.

Now the gods, who are embroiled in the conflict too, grow angry because Hector's body has not been buried. Finally they intervene by sending Hermes, their wing-footed messenger, to resolve the impasse. Hermes, who can travel between worlds, represents the ability to bridge the gap between seemingly implacable foes. In his role as guide of souls, he travels to earth and enables the Trojan King Priam to enter the Greek camp and plead for the release of his son's body. Once Achilles and Priam meet, they do the reconciling work themselves. Moved by Priam's courage and their common grief, Achilles finally relents and allows the old king to bear Hector's body back to Troy. Something shifts in his heart and he is able to let go of his pathological grief. When Hector is finally given *his* rites of burning, the events of history begin to unfold again.

In *The Odyssey*, a plea for proper burial appears in Book Eleven, aptly titled "A Gathering of Shades." The Greek warrior Odysseus, now at the midpoint of his journey home from Troy to Ithaca, has reached a critical juncture. He has taken refuge on Circe's island, where she tells him that he can go no further until he visits the underworld to consult the blind seer Tiresias. In psychological terms, we could say that on his individuation journey, the hero has exhausted his considerable ego strength and must now open himself to the wisdom of the unconscious in the person of Tiresias, a Wise Old Man figure. While in the underworld, he encounters many other spirits as well. The first is the shade of one of his own men, Elpenor, who had fallen to his death and been left behind, unburied and unmourned. With these words the young man implores Odysseus to give him his proper rites of burial:

> O my lord, remember me, I pray,
> do not abandon me unwept, unburied,
> to tempt the gods' wrath, while you sail for home; but fire my corpse, and all the gear I had—
> and build a cairn for me above the breakers—
> an unknown sailor's mark for men to come.
> Heap up a mound there, and implant upon it
> the oar I pulled in life with my companions.[5]

Elpenor understands that it is time for him to leave his body behind and join the company of shades. But he cannot do so without the aid of his former companions, and so they perform the rites he has requested, building a funeral pyre and weeping while his body burns, then fixing his oar upon his mound as he requested. Building the cairn and planting the oar upon it is a creative act that will remind future generations of their companion's unfortunate fate. In this episode, Elpenor and Odysseus have the psychological awareness to realize that unexpressed grief is detrimental to both the living and the dead. After performing Elpenor's burial rites, Odysseus and his men can proceed on their homeward voyage unburdened by guilt and remorse.

Odysseus has another encounter with a spirit of the dead in Hades when he meets the shade of his mother, who had died after he left Ithaca on his voyage to Troy. Since he did not know about her death, he is overcome with grief when he sees her. He is even more grief-stricken when she tells him that her loneliness for him had hastened her death. He tries three times to embrace her, but she goes "sifting through [his] hands, impalpable / as shadows are, and wavering like a dream."[6] When he asks if he is hallucinating, his mother reassures him that he is not losing his mind. But once the bodies of the dead have been burned, she says, the living can no longer embrace them and feel the relief of "welling tears."[7] Then, knowing that he will want to honor her when he returns to Ithaca, she bids him to "[n]ote all things strange / seen here, to tell your lady in after days."[8] In other words, he can elevate her and the other shades to archetypal status by telling their stories. What has died as history can be reborn as story, if he does the creative work of reanimating the shades of the dead as living images.

In addition to their meaning for individuals, funeral rites can move communities beyond their collective grief. Such ceremonies are as psychologically powerful today as they were 3,000 years ago. We see this power in memorial services for victims of accidents, natural disasters, and acts of violence and terrorism, and in the funerals of political figures, royalty, spiritual leaders, and even movie stars and music icons. Today our understanding of the afterlife is quite different from what it was in Homer's time. We no longer picture the dead living in a shadowy realm presided over by Hades and Persephone. Many of us do not believe in an afterlife at all. But in our hearts we know that our departed loved ones need our help to "cross over" into the realm of death, and that we begin to heal when we are able to weep for them, give them their proper rites of passage, and create memorials in their honor.

"Remember me!" *Hamlet*

Shakespeare's *Hamlet* is another great work that includes the presence of a ghost. In fact the play opens with a visitation by the ghost of the dead King Hamlet, and all the play's subsequent action turns upon that initial encounter with a spirit from the netherworld. As in Homer's work, the ghost requests a tribute—but in this case it is not a funeral rite, a monument, or a story. Instead, the ghost begs his son, also named Hamlet, to avenge his death, and declares that he (the ghost) will not find rest until his demand for justice has been fulfilled.

According to the best estimates, *Hamlet* was written in 1601, the year in which Shakespeare's father died, and five years after the death of the poet's eleven-year-old son, Hamnet, in 1596. This connection was not lost on Freud, who comments on it in *The Interpretation of Dreams*:

> I observe in a book on Shakespeare by Georg Brandes (1896) a statement that Hamlet was written immediately after the death of Shakespeare's father (in 1601), that is, under the immediate impact of his bereavement and, as we may well assume, while his childhood feelings about his father had been freshly revived. It is known, too, that Shakespeare's own son who died at an early age bore the name of "Hamnet," which is identical with "Hamlet."[9]

It may very well be that Shakespeare's mourning for his father and his son is reflected in Hamlet's grief. In fact, *Hamlet* has much to say about grief in all its forms, from Hamlet's "trappings and... suits of woe" (1.2.86), to the king and queen's lack of them, to Ophelia's madness and suicide following the death of her father, to Laertes's oath of revenge for his father's death and headlong leap into his sister Ophelia's grave. As a keen observer of human nature, and as one who had experienced grief himself, Shakespeare was intimately acquainted with the many human responses to loss.

As the play opens, the ghost of King Hamlet tells his son that he did not die a natural death, but was poisoned by his brother, Claudius, who then usurped his throne and married his queen, Gertrude. Naturally, the murdered king does not want this crime to go unpunished, and so he pleads with his son to avenge his death by killing Claudius. But he leaves it to Hamlet to devise the means of accomplishing his revenge, leaving him with the words, "Adieu, adieu! Hamlet, remember me!"[10] After such an experience, how could Hamlet forget? But he soon discovers that obeying his father's command is no easy matter. Immediately he is beset with doubts about the ghost. Is it real, or a figment of his imagination? Should he believe it? How can he verify what really happened? If he decides to kill his uncle, how and when should he do it? What about his mother? How much does she know? If he murders Claudius at prayer, will he send him straight to heaven? In fact, Hamlet thinks so much about his task that he is unable to do it until the final moments of the play. In terms of Jung's psychological types, one might say that he is an introverted intuitive thinking type who is so affected by his fertile imagination and conflicted emotions that he has trouble mobilizing his thinking function to arrive at a decision.

As a literary work, *Hamlet* speaks to modern audiences because its main character thinks and feels like a person of today and finds himself in a contemporary dilemma. When confronted by dreams and visions of the dead, we are just as terrified and confused as Hamlet, and we respond in much the same way. Are we hallucinating? Have we gone crazy? What do these apparitions mean? Should we listen to them and follow their instructions? What will others think of us if we do? What will happen if we don't? Like Hamlet, a student of philosophy, we are trained to think analytically and to determine the truth by weighing empirical evidence. Whatever cannot be verified experimentally is relegated to the trash heap of nonsense, superstition, or self-deception. We are also trained to doubt our feeling values and to distrust the knowledge of the heart. In this epistemological context, Hamlet's encounter with his father's ghost is like a nightmare that haunts the dreamer with a terrible truth. Intuitively, Hamlet "knows" more than he really wants to know about his father's death, and the ghost's appearance only confirms his previous suspicions. But because he cannot act on his father's orders at first, he "acts" in other ways, by playing stupid, pretending to be mad, and arranging the performance of a play-within-a-play to "catch the conscience of the King."[11] As Hamlet entangles himself in these machinations, the ghost appears again to remind him of his "almost blunted purpose."[12] This second apparition is like a recurring dream in which the same figure, with the same message, keeps showing up until the dreamer finally "gets it" and listens to what the unconscious is trying to say. By now Hamlet has established his uncle's guilt and has learned to verify his hunches, weigh his options, and trust own responses to a complex moral situation. Finally he succeeds in killing his uncle, but many others, including his mother, are poisoned as well, and Hamlet himself sustains a mortal wound. Before he dies, he becomes conscious of his role in history and understands that his own death is not without meaning. Only his best friend, Horatio, knows the full truth of his story, so with his dying breath Hamlet implores him:

> If thou didst ever hold me in thy heart,
> Absent thee from felicity a while
> And in this harsh world draw thy breath in pain
> To tell my story.[13]

When Horatio tells Hamlet's story to Fortinbras, the new king, the ghost's imperative, "Remember me!" finally brings healing rather than revenge. Hamlet knows that the health of the state depends upon a full and accurate account of the truth.

And so Horatio tells his story, not only to pay tribute to Hamlet, but also to guard the state against further contamination by the evil that had infected it in the first place.

In Shakespeare's time, the existence of the afterlife and the presence of ghosts were accepted without question. But there were thought to be good spirits and bad spirits, so Hamlet had to establish that the ghost was really the image of his dead father and not an evil goblin trying to drag him down to hell. The ghost was not a dream image, but a vision that Hamlet saw and heard with his physical senses. Other characters in the play saw it too, thus corroborating its reality. Today, such a vision might well be dismissed as a psychotic hallucination. The distinction between dream images, apparitions, and hallucinations is a subtle, but important one. In general, the content of dreams is similar to that of waking visions, but dreamers are unconscious, while visionaries are aware that they are encountering a dream-like apparition. People suffering from psychotic hallucinations are unable to differentiate literal from symbolic reality, and usually experience concurrent symptoms such as delusional thinking and affective disturbances. Whether the ghost in *Hamlet* is an actual apparition or a symbolic representation of Hamlet's intuition, the young prince is sane enough to verify the ghost's story by taking its message seriously and measuring its claims against the evidence of objective reality. This approach would have been just as valid if the ghost had appeared in a dream. In either case, obedience to the ghost's plea to "Remember me!" changes not only Hamlet's fate, but the course of history.

The art of elegy

The Iliad, *The Odyssey*, and *Hamlet* demonstrate literature's power to portray the complex relationship between the living and the dead. These great works include elements of elegy, a genre that includes music, sculpture, writing, painting, dance, and poetry. The term "elegy" is derived from the Greek word *elegos*, meaning "song of mourning."[14] It channels the emotions of grief into aesthetic form, connects the individual mourner to other bereaved souls, and relates personal loss to the archetypal level of reality. Elegy captures the incomparable uniqueness of those who have died and transforms them into living imaginal figures. We do not know exactly how elegy originated, but it may well have begun when mournful weeping evolved into formal chant and song. Rilke's "First Duino Elegy" hints that music began with Orpheus's mourning for Linos, an ancient vegetation god.[15] Orpheus is the legendary poet and musician who descended to the underworld to retrieve his dead wife, Eurydice. He convinced Hades to restore her to life, but at the last minute he failed to bring her back because he defied Hades's order not to turn around and look at her as they ascended. Perhaps his cry of grief at that moment was heard again as he wept for Linos, the god who was ritually mourned each year to guarantee that the crops would grow again in the spring.

Musical elegy features prominently in *The Death Rituals of Rural Greece*, mentioned in Chapter 4.[16] At the time of its publication in 1982, Greek village women mourned their dead in all-night vigils, daily visits to the cemetery, the lighting of lamps and candles, and the singing of laments. Five years after burial, the bones of the dead were exhumed, sprinkled with wine, and placed in the village ossuary. Then the entire community assembled in the church courtyard, where food was distributed and money collected to set up a memorial to the deceased. The day ended with mourners gathering in the bereaved family's home for more food and a final tribute. The next day the female relatives of the deceased would return to the cemetery to fill in the recently opened grave.[17] Funeral laments were at the center of these rituals, from the moment of death to the exhumation and relocation of the bones. Some laments were traditional, but many were created to honor a specific individual. This is part of a lament for Eleni, a young woman who died far from home in a hit-and-run auto accident:

> My mother is weeping for me with pain and with tears.
> My brothers and sisters are weeping for me with pain and with tears.[18]

As a mother who had also lost a daughter in a hit-and-run accident, I could easily imagine standing beside Eleni's grave with her mother and the other women of the village. I could share their grief, and I knew that if they could hear my story, they would share mine.

Elegy takes many forms in addition to music. Not long after Elizabeth's death, I found at her grave a small sculpture fashioned from a piece of driftwood and adorned with hanging feathers and shells. The dried skeleton of a tiny seahorse rested at the juncture of the two main branches of the driftwood. (Elizabeth had been fascinated by seahorses.) I rarely saw other people at the cemetery, but I knew they had been there because the sculpture was a bit different each time I visited. Marbles, stones, pottery, and more shells and feathers were soon added to it. Some offerings were humorous: one day a funny Valentine appeared, and in the summer there was a pair of sunglasses. I do not recall every item, but the whimsical beauty of the memorial touched me. I began to look forward to my visits to the cemetery, and eventually I contributed a few items—a pottery bowl, a blue marble, a flower or two—to the treasure trove. I felt that I belonged to a community of mourners who were engaged in a loving and playful nonverbal conversation with Elizabeth and with each other. Eventually I learned that her friend Chris Slay had made the sculpture, and was able to thank him for his soulful gift.

Unfortunately, this story does not end well. One day I arrived at the cemetery to discover that the driftwood sculpture had vanished. Dead flowers and plants were routinely cleared away from graves by the maintenance crew, but distinctive offerings such as this one were usually left for families to remove at their discretion. I found a groundskeeper and asked him what had happened. With a look of regret, he said that certain visitors (he did not say who, and I did not ask) had

Figure 8.1 Driftwood sculpture by Chris Slay, 1988
Photograph by the author.

objected to the memorial, which they regarded as a pagan symbol or even a sign of witchcraft. They had complained and the sculpture had been removed, by whom I do not know. I was shocked, saddened, and furious at the benighted souls who had misunderstood this work of art and had either asked for it to be taken down or dismantled it themselves, without bothering to inform our family. Fortunately I had taken pictures of it, but they were a poor substitute for the real thing. In the midst of my anger, however, I could imagine Elizabeth shrugging her shoulders as if to say, "Don't worry about it, Mom—they just don't get it, but you do!"

Another example of an elegiac sculpture appeared on a postcard sent to me by a friend who knew I had lost a child. The image on the card is a bronze head of Christ from Coventry Cathedral in England, created by a woman named Helen Huntington Jennings from the wreckage of the automobile in which her son had died. In the image, Christ's eyes are closed and a metal crown of thorns encircles his head. He looks peaceful but sorrowful, as though he has accepted his fate but grieves for those who mourn him. By creating this poignant sculpture, Mrs. Jennings found a way to express her grief, pay tribute to her son, and find meaning in her loss. When I look at the image, I see her own sorrow and courage reflected in the face of Christ.

In 1998, Anne McCracken and Mary Semel published an anthology entitled *A Broken Heart Still Beats: After Your Child Dies.* Both authors had lost a son and had found solace in in the works of writers who had also lost a child. As McCracken states:

> Mary and I have come to believe that comfort, such as it is, derives from recognizing that others before us, many others, have felt this very pain, struggled with the same questions, and reluctantly given up the lives they too had counted on. In this sense, misery does love company. It's not that we'd wish this pain on anyone, not Winston Churchill or Samuel Clemens, who both lost daughters; or Robert Frost, who, incredibly, lost four of his six children. However, we do welcome the painful truth that they were once as devastated as we, and yet found the courage to stay productive in this world. That Robert Frost got out of bed every morning, let alone wrote notable poetry, is nothing short of inspiring.[19]

Although they did not set out to write a book, McCracken and Semel soon realized that an anthology was taking shape in their hands—"a book we wish had been on the shelves when we needed it."[20] I wished the same thing. The book's twelve sections, arranged thematically, include authors from Sophocles to Shakespeare, Dostoevsky to Anne Morrow Lindbergh. As I read the various selections, I was astounded to learn how many writers, having suffered the death of a child, were able to find words to express their grief. In his sonnet "Surprised by Joy," William Wordsworth remonstrates with himself for forgetting, even for an instant, that his four-year-old daughter Catharine was dead:

> Surprised by joy—impatient as the Wind
> I turned to share the transport—Oh! With whom
> But thee, deep buried in the silent tomb,
> That spot which no vicissitude can find?
> Love, faithful love, recalled thee to my mind—
> But how could I forget thee? Through what power,
> Even for the least division of an hour,
> Have I been so beguiled as to be blind
> To my most grievous loss?—That thought's return
> Was the worst pang that sorrow ever bore,
>
> Save one, one only, when I stood forlorn,
> Knowing my heart's best treasure was no more;
> That neither present time, nor years unborn
> Could to my sight that heavenly face restore.[21]

Wordsworth's poem brings to mind a moment, several months after Elizabeth's death, when I forgot for an instant that she had died, and wanted to share something with her—a song, a funny anecdote, a bit of news, I don't remember what. The second that I realized, not only that she was dead, but that I had *forgotten* she was dead, was a terrible epiphany. How could I forget, "even for the least division of an hour"? In fact that moment may have marked a turning point, a moment when my feeling of loss no longer occupied every waking minute of my day and every nook and cranny of my psyche. In that instant I became aware of a new sort of guilt—the guilt of forgetting, which felt like abandonment of the one I loved so dearly. I had no words for it, but Wordsworth captured its poignancy in fourteen brief lines of poetry.

Jungian analysts Geri Grubbs and Charlotte Mathes, who are mentioned in previous chapters, found words to honor their sons and reach out to other bereaved families by writing their books. Grubbs includes her own grief dreams and the stories of three other bereaved parents whose dreams guided them through the mourning process. Mathes recounts her own story and those of other women dealing with "mother grief." She also offers insights about the healing function of creative work such as painting, gardening, and bricolage. For her, the Egyptian myth of Isis and the archetypal image of the Pietà, the Virgin Mary cradling her dead son in her lap, provided meaning and offered consolation.

Living memorials

Another form of tribute translates grief into living memorials. For example, Mothers Against Drunk Driving (MADD) was founded by Candy Lightner after the death of her thirteen-year-old daughter Cari in a hit-and-run accident in 1980. It now has hundreds of chapters across the U.S. and Canada and has supported the passage of stricter legislation to prevent alcohol-related automobile accident deaths. Elizabeth's friend Michael's mother became active in MADD and told his story many times at DUI classes, hoping to prevent similar tragedies. For many years I contributed to MADD myself by supporting its annual "tie one on" campaign, in which participants tie a red holiday ribbon to the antenna of their vehicle in memory of a loved one killed by a drunk driver.

Another memorial was created by Julie Nicholson, an Anglican priest whose daughter Jenny died in the London subway bombings of 2005. Unable to "reconcile her priestly function with her refusal to forgive the killers," Nicholson remained a priest but resigned her parish position.[22] In 2011 she published a book, *A Song for Jenny*, which was adapted into a BBC movie in 2015. Like Charlotte Mathes, Julie Nicholson found meaning in the image of the Pietà. Standing near the thin place of her daughter's death, she felt that she had been able to cradle Jenny at last. "I feel that on a spiritual and emotional level I have cradled her," she said. "I have expressed what I needed to express of the Pietà."[23]

A final example of a living memorial was created by Pam and Randy Cope, a couple whose fifteen-year-old son, Jantsen, died of a heart ailment in 1999.

In his memory, the Copes founded "Touch a Life Ministry," which assists children in Vietnam, Cambodia, and Ghana. They have also adopted two Vietnamese orphans themselves. Thus, the ministry created to honor their son has filled their lives with new challenges, new people, and new meaning. Pam Cope has told her story in a book entitled *Jantsen's Gift: A True Story of Grief, Rescue, and Grace.*[24]

A time of famine

Funeral rites, memorials, elegies, and books spring from the impulse to give form to the experience of grief and to impart ongoing life to the dead. But after these creative projects have been completed, a mood of depression and despair can follow. This is Demeter's state of mind after she fails to immortalize Demophoon. Taking no pleasure in her beautiful shrine, she blights the earth with a famine, a symbol of the barrenness in her heart. As the first anniversary of Elizabeth's death approached, I felt a similar famine in my psyche. I had returned to Zürich and resumed my studies, but had little energy for the work required to complete my training. I was not actively suicidal, but at times I thought that it would be all right to die. Then, in this bleak season, I had a dream in which I journeyed to the underworld and witnessed a ritual of death and rebirth. This powerful dream, which also contained hints of new life, is the subject of the next chapter.

Notes

1 C. G. Jung, "Psychological Commentary," in *The Tibetan Book of the Dead*, xxxv–lii.
2 Homer, "Hymn to Demeter," 12–15.
3 D. W. Winnicott, *Playing and Reality*, 4.
4 Homer, "A Friend Consigned to Death," in *The Iliad of Homer*, 537–538.
5 Homer, "A Gathering of Shades," in *The Odyssey*, 187.
6 *Ibid.*, 191.
7 *Ibid.*
8 *Ibid.*, 192.
9 S. Freud, *The Interpretation of Dreams*, 299.
10 W. Shakespeare, *Hamlet*, 1.5.91.
11 *Ibid.*, 2.2.634.
12 *Ibid.*, 3.4.111.
13 *Ibid.*, 5.2.357–360.
14 Merriam-Webster's Collegiate Dictionary, 10th ed., s.v. "elegy."
15 R. M. Rilke, *Duino Elegies*, 26.
16 L. M. Danforth and A. Tsiaras, *The Death Rituals of Rural Greece*, 1982.
17 In an e-mail dated November 6, 2008, Alexander Tsiaras wrote, "The village I focused on was a village called Paliokastro. This is my mother's village. It

is still there but has modernized and many of these rituals have disappeared or been reduced in their degree of execution."

18 *Ibid.*, 115.
19 A. McCracken and M. Semel, eds., *A Broken Heart Still Beats: After Your Child Dies*, xxviii.
20 *Ibid.*, xxvii.
21 W. Wordsworth, "Surprised by Joy," in *The Poetical Works of Wordsworth*, 204.
22 Alan Cowell, "A Suicide Bomb, a Dead Daughter and a Test of Faith," in *The New York Times*, May 6, 2006.
23 *Ibid.*
24 P. Cope with A. Molloy, *Jantsen's Gift: A True Story of Grief, Rescue, and Grace,* 2009.

Chapter 9

Descent to the underworld

The night-sea journey

In the life of the psyche, Demeter's desire for revenge might correspond to an emotional breakdown in which toxic rage overwhelms the ego. The wrath of Achilles after the death of Patroclus, discussed in the previous chapter, is another instance of this psychic state. In this dark time, suicidal and homicidal fantasies are probably more common than we like to admit. We may rage against ourselves, telling ourselves that we could have saved our loved ones and that we don't want (or deserve) to live if they are dead. Or we may seek to punish those who did not save them (or who inadvertently contributed to their deaths) by filing lawsuits or seeking excessive financial damages. On the other hand, we may be plunged into the lassitude of depression, like Hamlet after his father's death. The barren state of the earth in the Homeric Hymn reflects a condition in which the wellsprings of libido, or psychic energy, dry up and cease to flow. Concerned about our rage or inertia, well-meaning friends may advise us to "get over it" and "get on with our lives." But the truth is that we are not ready or able to put ourselves back together yet. Like Demeter, Achilles, and Hamlet, whose archetypal stories mirror our own struggles, we must endure a dark time before we can return to life again.

As the first anniversary of Elizabeth's death approached, I found myself trying to put the pieces of my life back together. Occasionally I had flare-ups of anger, but most often I was aware of depressive symptoms such as lack of energy, a greater than usual need for solitude, and little appetite for enjoyment. Then, in the midst of this barren time, I had this dream:

> I go down into the underworld, the land of the dead. A male guide leads me there and shows me around. I watch as bodies are put into a big common box or tank. As new bodies arrive, the old ones are covered and turned over in a kind of composting process. The guide says that the dead keep each other warm in this box. Then they are moved to another place and he makes holes in their skulls to allow the matter inside to come out. He tells me that the skulls would swell up and burst if he did not do this.

Elizabeth's body is in the box with several others. I feel horrified as I watch her corpse undergo the composting and skull-piercing process. Finally she emerges from the box. She is alive again and I can talk to her. As in other dreams, I am crying because I'm so glad to see her again. She looks like herself except that her hair is dyed black—but a bit of her blonde hair is shining through. She says that she is sorry for being careless on the night she died and that she didn't mean to hurt me or anyone else. Then she tells me that there is something I can do for her. Looking me right in the eye, she says, "Tell people about me." I take this to mean that she wants other young people to know what happened to her so that they will be more careful than she was.

In this dream, the motif of the descent to the underworld linked my personal experience of grief to the archetypal dimension of mourning. In myth and literature, as in dreams, the underworld is a symbol of what Jung called the "collective unconscious," the motifs and patterns of behavior that are common to all humanity, but are usually inaccessible to consciousness. The journey to the underworld represents the ego's descent into these depths, from which it emerges with a new orientation to life. Jung refers to this descent as the *nekyia*, or night-sea journey. In it, the hero (who represents the individuating ego) undergoes literal or symbolic death and is later reborn into newness of life.[1] Jung's own *nekyia*, his "confrontation with the unconscious," occurred after his break with Freud in 1912. After tracking the pattern in his own life, he identified it as a crucial stage in the journey of individuation, "the process by which a person becomes a psychological 'individual,' that is, a separate, indivisible unity or 'whole.'"[2] Jung's *Red Book*, or *Liber Novus*, portrays in words and images his own experience of the night-sea journey.[3]

In *The Hero with a Thousand Faces*, Joseph Campbell depicts the journey to the underworld as an essential feature of the heroic quest, or "monomyth."[4] As he demonstrates, the passage through Hades is a major theme in world mythology. The biblical story of Jonah, the Egyptian myth of Osiris, and even the tale of Pinocchio, the wooden marionette who longed to be a real boy, reveal the universal nature of the hero's descent into the underworld. In an ancient Sumerian myth, the goddess Inanna descends to the netherworld, is divested of her "magnificent regalia," dies, and is hung on a meat hook to rot.[5] Finally, with the help of Enki, the god of wisdom, she is resurrected and returns to earth. In Greek mythology, as we have seen, Orpheus travels to Hades to fetch his wife, Eurydice, and Odysseus descends to the underworld to consult with Tiresias. In the Christian tradition, Jesus descends into Hell in the three days between his death and resurrection. And in *The Divine Comedy*, Dante writes about his midlife descent into the Inferno, his journey through Purgatory, and his final ascent into Paradise. In these tales, heroes and heroines suffer actual or symbolic death and return to the world of consciousness with a new relationship to the higher powers that shape their destiny.

If the night-sea journey represents the process of individuation, it is also an apt symbol of the mourning process. Like individuation, mourning involves regression into chaotic emotions, disorganized thinking, and frightening visions and dreams. The loss of orientation and control feels like death—and for the ego, that is precisely what it is. Grief shakes the ego, tears it apart, scatters the pieces, and then gathers and re-forms them into an entirely new structure. The bereaved person who emerges from this ordeal is very different from the one who descended into it. After enduring this shattering experience, one cannot simply return to the world and resume "normal" life.

The guide of souls

The archetypal figure of the *psychopomp*, or guide of souls, plays an essential role in the night-sea journey. Often the guide is a Wise Old Man figure like Philemon, whom Jung encountered during his confrontation with the unconscious. As Murray Stein notes in his book *In Midlife*, the Wise Old Man represents "the ability to see beyond surfaces to what is invisible or unconscious for others... [He] represents knowledge of unconscious patterns and facts; his vision is directed toward the invisible, toward psyche."[6] Enki is a Wise Old Man figure in the tale of Inanna, while Tiresias fulfills this role in *The Odyssey*. In *The Divine Comedy*, Virgil guides Dante through Hell and Purgatory and then departs so that Beatrice can lead him to Paradise.

Beatrice is an example of a feminine guide of souls, as are Calypso, Circe, Athena and other feminine figures in *The Iliad* and *The Odyssey*. If the Wise Old Man represents inward-turning vision, the feminine guide embodies the ability to *relate* to inner events. When Jung defines the anima as "the principle of relatedness," he is referring to the experience of feeling "animated" by what transpires in the inner world. The anima guides the ego into a feeling relationship with the ideas and images that emerge from dreams, fantasies, and other contents of the unconscious.[7] Without the ability to relate to this material, the ego is like a spectator at a play, observing the drama but not touched by it. The characters may be noble, the action lively, and the outcome dramatic—but the ego is not affected by them and therefore cannot experience transformation. Jung's first image of his own anima in *The Red Book* was the figure of a beautiful young blind woman named Salome, who functioned as a companion to Philemon. At first Jung did not trust her, but eventually he formed a relationship with her and learned to ask for her help in translating his unruly emotions into images. After many years of practice, he learned to "see" the images himself and no longer needed her assistance. In other words, he gradually integrated his anima into his ego structure.

Like Dante and Jung, Demeter has both female and male guides as she searches for Persephone. Hecate, the ancient goddess of crossroads, the underworld, and witches, represents the intuitive ability to see in the dark and discern the hidden nature of things. She leads Demeter to the Sun, a masculine god who represents the light of clear and focused consciousness. Together the two guides confirm that Persephone has been carried into the underworld, and this knowledge precipitates Demeter into an underworld experience of her own.

In actual life, a therapist, analyst, or spiritual director may take the role of guide. A trusted friend or relative may become a companion on the path of mourning, or a guide may appear in a dream, as in my experience. (I was fortunate to have two wise and compassionate analysts who also served as guides.) My dream guide's image is indistinct and I do not identify him with a specific person or figure. But it is his job to show me the dead bodies, describe the composting process, perform the skull-piercing operation, and explain why it is necessary. This he does in a matter-of-fact tone, suggesting that he is so used to his job that the horror of it no longer disturbs him. He reminds me of the gravedigger in *Hamlet*, of whom Horatio says, "Custom hath made it in him a property of easiness."[8] The gravedigger regards death with a matter-of-fact, no-nonsense attitude and points to the bones he uncovers as a reminder of the end awaiting all living things. In his role as guide, he has the task of normalizing death, a task which he accomplishes by joking and singing about it. At first Hamlet is shocked at the gravedigger's light-hearted attitude, but their conversation jars him loose from his obsessive brooding and frees him to take the action necessary to bring his conflict to a final resolution. This movement from depression to action, from grief to mourning, could not have been achieved without the guidance of the gravedigger in the unlikely role of a clown.

The alchemy of death

Returning to my dream, the images of the bodies in the box and the skulls being pierced led me to review Jung's interest in alchemy, the medieval art which he interpreted as a symbolic representation of the process of individuation. After years of analyzing ancient alchemical texts, he concluded that the alchemists had projected their own quest for wholeness onto certain physical elements and operations. Of course, we know today that it is not possible to transform lead into gold, as the alchemists hoped to do. Nevertheless, alchemical images and symbols appear with surprising frequency in contemporary fantasies, visions, and dreams. My dream of the underworld contained several allusions to the initial stage of the alchemical process known as the *nigredo* or "blackening." As described by Edward Edinger in *Anatomy of the Psyche*, this phase includes the processes of *mortificatio* and *putrefactio*, which have to do with "darkness, defeat, torture, mutilation, death, and rotting."[9] To begin the alchemical process, lead, dirt, or other base material (known as the *prima materia*) was sealed in the alchemical vessel and subjected to heat, distillation, and other chemical operations. In psychological terms, the *prima materia* refers to the elemental emotions, chaotic thoughts, frightening dreams, and strange fantasies that emerge during individuation and mourning.

In mourning, the *nigredo* can involve the "blackening" of the idealized image of the deceased. By this time I had already dreamed several times of visiting the scene of the accident and feeling angry at Elizabeth. Those dreams initiated the *nigredo* by focusing on the reality of her death, raising my "negative" emotions to consciousness, and calling attention to her human shortcomings. The dream of the underworld turned up the heat by forcing me to watch dead bodies (including hers) being tossed into a big box (a variant of the alchemical vessel), covered, and turned over. I could feel the "blackening" of consciousness as the gruesome images registered in my mind. They reminded me of the last scene in the film *Amadeus*, in which Mozart's body is dumped into a mass grave and covered with lime like all the rest. Whether his body was actually buried in this way or not, the scene is a vivid reminder of the end that awaits us all, no matter how bright and talented and creative we may be.

Another vivid image appears when the guide tells me that the dead keep each other warm in the box. Perhaps they are warmed by each other's company, but it is also true that heat is generated when dead organisms are undergoing the process of decay. In biological composting, heat is produced when organic matter is broken down into nutrient-rich loam, the desired end-product of the process. The guide's comment about the dead keeping each other warm indicates that just as Elizabeth's physical body is subject to decay, the body of my "dark" emotions and thoughts is experiencing a similar process.

Images of the head, skull, and hair figure prominently in this dream, as in several others. On the literal level, Elizabeth suffered a fatal head injury. But on the symbolic level, the dead head (*caput mortuum*), another symbol in the alchemical *opus*, refers to the residue left after the distillation of the *prima materia*. The rotting material inside the skulls is an image of "dead" psychic matter, such as outworn attitudes, obsolete images, and destructive emotions. Strong affects such as anger, envy, guilt, and the desire for revenge can ferment in the psyche, creating toxic matter that can swell up and explode in the form of obsessive thoughts, outbursts of rage, and impulsive violence. As he pierces the skulls of the dead, my guide explains that he is attempting to prevent this sort of explosion. It seems that he must penetrate the defenses that surround the psychic structure in order to preserve the psyche. This is the paradox of *mortificatio*: the psyche must be "pierced" in order to be healed. Boring holes in the skulls of the dead allows the *prima materia* to be released slowly and consciously, as it is in analysis, therapy, or spiritual direction. Once the emotional pressure is relieved, psychic energy can be channeled into life again. In this way the dead contents are transformed into gold, a symbol of the wholeness achieved at the end of the alchemical process.

After piercing the skulls, the guide fades out of the picture, for his work is done. Now Elizabeth emerges from the compost pit with dyed black hair and a remorseful attitude. Here the *prima materia* appears in the form of the black hair that grows from her head, I take this to mean that her dark thoughts (and mine) now take the form of separate strands that can be untangled and rearranged. My personal association to the black hair is a "fright wig" that Elizabeth used to wear as a joke. Grimacing like an old hag, she would pull it over her hair, dance around, and cackle like the Wicked Witch of the West. This was her playful way of acting out her own shadow and honoring the "witchy" part of her that was not, and did not want to be, kind, good, smart, beautiful, and well-behaved. Even as an adolescent, she was aware of the darker side of her personality. In the dream, her "dyed" black hair may indicate that something in her thinking—perhaps her naive belief in her own innocence and immortality—has "died." When she apologizes and says that she didn't mean to hurt anyone, my anger softens into compassion. Thus the *prima materia* becomes the "alchemical gold" of a new state of mind and heart for both of us. The gold shining through her black hair offers a glimpse of this development.

Alchemical gold

The image of gold shining through black hair brings two Brothers Grimm fairy tales to mind.[10] "Iron John" is the story of a young prince who frees a wild man (Iron John) imprisoned in his father's castle. The wild man leads the boy into the forest, shows him an enchanted spring, and instructs him not to touch the water. Of course, the curious youth cannot resist putting his finger and then his hair into the spring, whereupon both finger and hair turn to gold. For this "failure," (which actually represents a step towards independent thinking), the prince is banished from the forest and embarks upon a series of adventures, during which he slowly grows to manhood. During these years of trial, he hides his golden hair under a cap. His instinctual wisdom tells him that he is not yet ready to show his gold to the world. But on one occasion, when he thinks no one is looking, he pulls off his cap and the king's daughter sees his beautiful hair. Once his inner gold shines forth, he reveals himself as a prince, marries the princess, and together they inherit her father's kingdom.

In the second tale, "Snow White and Rose Red," a big black bear seeks shelter in the cottage of a widow and her two young daughters one winter night. They befriend him, play with him, and offer him a place to sleep by the fire. When spring comes, he tells them that he must leave to guard his treasure from a wicked dwarf who wants to steal it. As he goes out the door, his fur catches on the bolt and Snow White, the quiet sister, catches a glimpse of gold beneath his black coat. Later he kills the dwarf and is revealed as a prince clad completely in gold. He marries Snow White, his brother marries Rose Red, and along with their mother they all live happily ever after in his castle.

In both tales, early glimpses of gold hint that the process of psychological transformation, or individuation, has begun. The hint of gold beneath Elizabeth's black hair in my dream indicates that an expansion of consciousness is underway, but is not yet complete. Her dream image and my relation to it are undergoing a profound alteration, as revealed in her changed attitude and mine. The dream indicates that both of us are facing the hard reality of her death and the possibility that new life may emerge from the compost pit of outworn attitudes, dark thoughts, and toxic emotions.

In his book on alchemy, Edinger cites a dream containing similar images of death and rebirth. In fact this is a complicated dream-within-a-dream, in which the dreamer is attending a party for a dead friend, who is relating a dream that he had before his death:

> Its major image was a great circle of grain standing 80 inches high. It grew out of a pit in the earth which contained dead bodies that were also buried treasure. [In the dream] the dead friend is trying to convey to his [living] friend the importance of the dream.[11]

This dream is accompanied by an image from *The Hermetic Museum*, in which a dead body lies beside an open grave, from which arise a resurrected body and a large sheaf of grain. According to Edinger, the dream occurred on Halloween, a thin time when the spirits of the dead are believed to walk abroad and make contact with the living. The dream figure of the dead friend places special emphasis on the grain growing from the pit in the earth, as if to suggest that the bodies of the dead, the "buried treasure," provide the compost that fertilizes new growth. The dream and the image reminded me of my initial dream, in which Elizabeth said, "Let your tears fertilize my ground." Both dreams suggest that the operation of *mortificatio* transforms dead bodies, fertilized by the tears of grief, into the "buried treasure" from which new life is born.

A new guide of souls

In my dream, as in many others, I wept with joy to see Elizabeth again. But this time I did not embrace her, for I felt that she had moved beyond the corporal world into the purely imaginal realm. When she looked into my eyes and said, "Tell people about me," I thought at first that she wanted me to warn other young people to be more careful and avoid her fate. But later I realized that I could also honor her by telling my dreams—not to dramatize my grief or to immortalize her, but to communicate what mourning has taught me about the objective psyche and the ongoing connection between the living and the dead. In the early stages of grief, when sorrow is all-consuming, we cling to our memories of our loved ones as they existed in time and space. As memory dims, however, they fade into "shades" of their former selves. But when they appear in our dreams, their images take on new life and inform our imagination with their presence. When Elizabeth first appeared in my dreams, I associated her image with her historical presence and felt that I was granting her a form of eternal life by holding her in my memory. But as time passed and her dream image took on a life of its own, I realized that her imaginal presence was enlarging my consciousness and altering my view of the "afterlife." Of course, I hold her in my memory and I always will. But my soul is also enriched by her imaginal presence. This is a gift that I did not imagine, a grace that I did not anticipate. It is the tender plant that springs from her ground, the gold that glitters beneath her coal-black hair.

In *The Divine Comedy*, Virgil departs when his work is completed, and Beatrice appears as Dante's new guide. Likewise, after explaining the composting process and releasing the *prima materia* from the skulls of the dead, the dream guide fades away and Elizabeth, transformed in the alchemical tomb, emerges as my new guide. In previous dreams, her image had already begun to function as a guide by encouraging me to weep, filling me with her breath, and teaching me about guardian angels. Here she expands the role by directing me to tell her story. Her words are not a request, but a command: "You must do this," she seems to be saying. "This is your task now. Take your sorrow and turn it into gold."

In our guiding myth, a guide also appears to reunite Demeter and Persephone. The next episode of the Homeric Hymn reveals how Zeus deploys Hermes, the messenger of the gods, to intercede with Hades and bring about a resolution of the gods' impasse. In the process of mourning, dreams often perform the same guiding and mediating function.

Notes

1 C. G. Jung, *Symbols of Transformation*, *CW* 5, § 308–311, 319, and 484.
2 C. G. Jung, *The Archetypes and the Collective Unconscious*, *CW* 9i, § 490.
3 C. G. Jung, *The Red Book* (*Liber Novus*).
4 J. Campbell, *The Hero with a Thousand Faces*.
5 S. B. Perera, *Descent to the Goddess*, 9.
6 M. Stein, *In Midlife: A Jungian Perspective*, 121.
7 For Jung's account of his relationship with the anima, see *Memories*, 210–212.
8 W. Shakespeare, *Hamlet*, 5.1.75–76.
9 E. F. Edinger, *Anatomy of the Psyche*, 149.
10 The Brothers Grimm, *The Complete Fairy Tales of the Brothers Grimm*, trans. Jack Zipes.
11 E. F. Edinger, *Anatomy of the Psyche*, 162.

Chapter 10

"You can visit them in their dreams!"

A divine dilemma

We now return to Homer's "Hymn to Demeter," where the goddess sits in her empty shrine, refusing to allow the crops to grow on earth. In the meantime Persephone is a prisoner in the underworld. Hades will not let her go, and her father Zeus finds himself in the position of a reluctant mediator between his stubborn brother and sister. In the Greek pantheon, Demeter, Hades, and Zeus are siblings, each with authority over a separate domain. Persephone, sometimes called the "Kore," represents the promise of new life and embodies the union of Zeus and Demeter, heaven and earth. The problem is that Demeter wants her to remain a maiden, an eternal girl who will never marry and bear children of her own. Zeus knows that Demeter's wish is untenable, and so he turns a blind eye when Hades seizes his daughter and forces her to become his wife. Hades, for his part, is a possessive husband who does not want to release his bride. In other words, he wants to hoard her beauty in the underworld, preventing new life from emerging on earth. In the power struggle between him and Demeter, there is real danger of an intractable conflict in which life will come to a standstill and both humans and gods will be destroyed.

In psychological terms, the gods' predicament reflects an impasse in which new creative energy has come into being but remains in the unconscious (the underworld) and is unable to take earthly form. A depression may keep it from reaching fruition, or it may need to incubate for a season before emerging into the light of day. In developmental terms, this dynamic might be reflected in a situation in which parents and children refuse to move beyond psychological fusion into a more mature relationship. One parent (in Persephone's case, the father) may support the child's maturation, but in attempting to foster it, he or she may incur the other parent's wrath. In terms of family dynamics, the dilemma resembles a codependent relationship between an adult child and his or her conflicted parents. The child may continue to look to them for physical, emotional, and financial support, while they are at odds with each other about how to provide it (or whether to provide it at all). In this state, a young person is unable to leave adolescence behind and grow into full adulthood. Even after leaving home, starting a career, marrying, and having children, he or she may remain an emotional child. On the collective level, this situation may arise when a group, state, or nation is split by conservative and progressive forces, as in the world today. This "tension of opposites," as Jung would call it, must be endured until a compromise is reached or a "reconciling symbol" emerges to transcend the impasse.[1]

Zeus, seeing the gravity of the situation, now realizes that it is time for him to act. But an earlier agreement with his siblings prohibits them from encroaching on each other's territory. Therefore he cannot intervene by visiting earth or descending to the underworld. He needs to come up with a plan that does not risk a direct confrontation with either Demeter or Hades.[2] In the structure of the psyche, Zeus symbolizes what Jung calls the Self, "the archetype of order, the totality of the personality."[3] In its negative aspect, this archetype appears as a need for rigid order and control. In mourning, a person in the grip of this energy would be inclined to suppress emotion, stay busy with a tight schedule of activities, and "move on" without giving due attention to their grief. On the other hand, the positive aspect of the father archetype would foster the appropriate expression of emotion, allow time and space for reflection, and accept the summons to explore the deeper meaning of mourning. This is the position Zeus takes when he sends messengers to appeal to the higher sensibilities of his grieving sister, Demeter, and his obstinate brother, Hades.

The messengers of the gods

The first envoy to be deployed is Zeus's personal messenger, Iris, goddess of the rainbow. She visits Demeter at her shrine in Eleusis, but Demeter will not to speak to her and sends her away. Not one to accept defeat, Zeus then sends all the gods to present gifts to his sister and beg her to reconsider. Now at least she speaks, but she is adamant that she will not set foot on Olympus or allow the crops to grow again until she is reunited with her daughter. In psychological terms, the soft words of Iris and the entreaties of the gods may represent the first whispers of an inner voice that tells the bereaved it is time to move beyond rage and depression and into life again. But Demeter is still too deeply entrenched in grief to listen. The crux of the problem remains in the underworld (the unconscious), where new life, in the figure of the Kore, is held prisoner and cannot escape. At this point in the story, another emissary is needed, one who can appeal directly to Hades. And so Zeus summons his son Hermes to travel to the underworld and convince Hades to release Persephone and guide her back to earth.

Hermes, messenger of the gods, is the quintessential symbol of the *psychopomp*, or guide of souls. With his winged feet and golden wand, he can travel between worlds and mediate between heaven, earth, and the underworld. He is able to slip in and out of keyholes, walk so softly that his feet seem not to touch the ground, and weave a net of elaborate deceptions to cover his tracks—all the while appearing as innocent as a newborn babe.[4] In psychological language, he represents the "transcendent function," the living symbol that connects consciousness to the unconscious and bridges the gap between conflicting forms of archetypal energy.[5] In actual life, the transcendent function may take the form of a novel idea, a surprising dream, or a spark of inspiration that reconciles opposing attitudes. In the myth of Demeter, the spark ignites when Hermes approaches Hades, who finally becomes reasonable and agrees to release Persephone. But before she leaves, sly Hades feeds her a pomegranate seed, knowing that whoever eats the fruit of the underworld will eventually have to return. Then Hermes, in his role as guide, escorts the young goddess back to earth, where she has a joyful reunion with her mother. Once the standoff between the gods is over, new life returns to the barren earth.

"You can visit them in their dreams!"

In the barren season of mourning, new life may emerge in the form of a potent dream that feels qualitatively different from those occurring before. Such dreams do not emphasize reunion, the traumatic events of death, or the dreamer's emotions, although these elements may still be present. Instead, the dead appear as emissaries, bringing new images and a new outlook to the dreamer. These dreams suggest that sprigs of new life are beginning to emerge from the "ground" of the psyche. The hints may come in the form of surprising—even humorous—images, reconciling symbols, and clear verbal messages. Whatever form they take, dreams of this kind reveal the imaginal figures of the dead in a new light.

About a year and a half after Elizabeth's death, I dreamed:

I'm in a house with Michael's mother and sister, sitting on the floor and playing with some small multicolored plastic balls. Some of the balls get lost in the carpet and we laugh, saying that they'll be turning up for years to come, like stale jellybeans after Easter.

Suddenly Elizabeth is there and starts to play with us, using the plastic forms to create amusing, whimsical animals and other creatures. I watch her and we talk to each other. Sometimes I ask her to repeat what she has just said, because I want to hear the sound of her voice again. While this is going on, I'm aware that I'm dreaming and that she is an image from the dream world. I feel that I need to hold my breath so as not to break the spell—that if I say anything, try to touch her, or acknowledge that this is a dream, the bubble will burst and she will disappear.

Then she goes outside and runs up to a fence, stands on the bottom rail, and greets a young man who runs up from the other side. As they lean over and kiss, I realize that he is Michael. He and Elizabeth come back to the house and I wonder how his mother will react, because I know that she is skeptical about the afterlife. But when she sees him, she receives him as if his sudden appearance is "no big deal," like one of the quick, unannounced visits he used to make during his lifetime.

Now Elizabeth goes outside again and finds an old car parked on the side of the street. It is a funny old rattletrap, patched together from many parts, with the rounded shape of a car from the 1940s or 50s. Elizabeth is delighted and gets right in. She is like a child with a new toy, and can't wait to go for a ride. She gets behind the wheel and "pretends" to drive, like little kids do. Michael and I get into the car too. Now he is driving, I'm in the passenger seat, and Elizabeth is in the back with her head resting on her arms on the back of the seat. The three of us are happy and excited as we drive along. Great trees with curving branches arch overhead. They look like the big elms that towered over the streets in the city where I grew up, before Dutch elm disease wiped them out. But these are ginkgo trees and their leaves are just beginning to turn yellow. I say to Elizabeth several times, "Look, look, the ginkgoes are turning!"

Then she introduces me to Michael, whom I have not yet met officially. He says that he's been wanting to meet me and give me a kiss. He's driving very casually, using one hand and not paying much attention to the road. I think he should be more careful, although I know he and Elizabeth are dead and beyond the reach of harm. When I see a truck approaching from the other direction I say, "Hey, watch where you're going!" But the car and truck pass each other with plenty of room to spare, and then Michael turns and we give each other a brief kiss on the lips. He says that he wishes he could visit his parents, because he knows that they miss him a lot. Elizabeth looks at him and says with much conviction (but with a twinkle in her eye), "Oh, but you can! You can visit them in their dreams!"

With this I wake up. The bubble has burst, but I'm left with the feeling that this is Elizabeth's way of affirming that she's been visiting me in my dreams. I want to go back to sleep so that I can visit with her some more. Between waking and sleeping, I "see" an image of water with a ferryboat upon which we can travel when we want to visit each other.

I include this dream in its entirety because it contains several new and unusual images: the colorful balls, the old patched-together car, and the tall golden-leafed trees. The world of the dream is a playful, colorful one, in which Elizabeth and Michael seem very much at home. In this thin place we are beyond time and space, floating together in the evanescent bubble of the dream state.

In this dream, as in my premonitory dream of the horses, the veil between this world and the next is gossamer-thin. But now the atmosphere is light and playful, rather than eerie and foreboding. The theme of play is introduced in the first scene, as I sit on the floor playing with Michael's mother and sister. Elizabeth's mood is playful as she joins us, greets and kisses Michael, discovers the old car, and jumps in for a ride. Michael seems happy too, and I am enjoying myself so much that I don't want the dream to end. Even Elizabeth's last comment, "You can visit them in their dreams," is said playfully, with a twinkle in her eye to let me know she is aware that she has been visiting me in mine. After the somber mood of many of my other grief dreams, the lighthearted tone of this one was an unanticipated and very welcome change.

The word "play," derived from "the Old English *pleg(i)an* 'to exercise', [and] *plega* 'brisk movement', [is] related to the Middle Dutch *pleien* 'leap for joy, dance'."[6] The word's origins suggest that play involves exhilarating and joyful activity. D. W. Winnicott, whose concept of the "transitional object" was introduced in Chapter 2, also explored the importance of play in human development. According to him, play occurs in the "transitional space" between subjective and objective reality, which he calls the realm of "illusion." He is not referring to belief in something that is not real, or to wishful thinking, but to an "intermediate area of experiencing, to which inner reality and external life both contribute."[7] As children play, at first with their mother's breast and then with a succession of soft objects, dolls, and toys, they gradually establish a connection with the outer world. The objects "given" or "found" in the world are also "created" by the child and take on symbolic value. Thus, the "intermediate area" described by Winnicott is the playground in which human creativity is nurtured and developed. The capacity for symbolic thinking originates here, as does the ability to combine and manipulate objects in unique and unusual ways. In adulthood, the intermediate area is "retained in the intense experiencing that belongs to the arts and to religion and to imaginative living, and to creative scientific work."[8] Dream space, too, is an "intermediate area" in which dream figures engage in playful, creative action. In my dream, the dream ego (the "I" in the dream) knows that Elizabeth and Michael are dead, and yet I greet them as figures who can play, talk, laugh, and joke with me in the bubble of the imaginal world. As long as I do not break the spell by acknowledging that I am dreaming, the "willing suspension of disbelief" sustains the transitional space in which the dream characters are engrossed in play.[9]

Like the events in a fairy tale, the action of this dream begins in ordinary space/time, but moves quickly into the imaginal realm. In the first scene of the dream, Michael's mother, sister, and I are sitting on the floor, just as children would, playing with an assortment of brightly colored plastic balls. The theme of loss and recovery is introduced in a light vein as we joke about finding the lost balls later, just as people find stale jellybeans around the house long after Easter is over. Since Michael's family is Jewish, they would not have celebrated this holiday. But there is a close connection between Easter and Passover, the ritual commemoration of Israel's liberation from bondage and exodus from Egypt. Both holidays center on the archetypal motif of death and rebirth in the midst of a dark, chaotic time. Jellybeans, brightly colored like the plastic balls and shaped like tiny eggs, represent the color and sweetness that return to life in moments of joy. The dream implies that these lost morsels of flavor and energy can be found in unusual places long after the day of Resurrection is over. Easter is not confined to one season, but can happen every day.

When the dream figure of Elizabeth enters the room, she introduces new energy that transforms an ordinary space into an extraordinary playground. She begins to fashion amusing animals and whimsical creatures from the plastic balls, all the while speaking a language that I cannot understand. I know that I am dreaming and that she is trying to convey a message, but the meaning of it appears to be in the objects she is creating, more than in her words. In association to the objects, I think of artists who have the vision, humor, and talent to create whimsical works of art from "found objects" such as plastic containers, buttons, old computer parts, hubcaps, metal, etc.—things commonly referred to as "junk." Recently I saw an exhibit of sculpture at the Smith College Art Museum in Northampton, Massachusetts, in which each work of art was fashioned entirely of discarded plastic bags, bottles, toys, tubing, buoys, and other so-called trash. Each piece was beautiful, surprising, and ingenious, demonstrating the limitless capacity of human creativity. In my dream Elizabeth puts the balls together using the same novel approach. She is full of creative energy and wants to demonstrate it and show us how to use it. In short, she is teaching us how to play.

In the next scene, the action of the dream moves from the house to the outer world. As in earlier dreams, the house symbolizes the inner world of psyche, in which images of the dead assume imaginal reality. But here the boundary between "inner" and "outer" is permeable and the figures move easily between the two. Within the bubble of the dream space, psyche produces many variations on the theme of the boundary. Even the image of the fence is a playful riff on the boundary motif. This dream world contains many spaces: the house where we play, the yard and fence where Elizabeth and Michael greet and kiss, the street where they discover the funny old car, the interior of the car itself, and the wide streets down which we drive. With the help of Elizabeth in her mercurial role as guide, we can visit them all.

In my dream of the underworld, Elizabeth emerged from the alchemical vessel and assumed the role of messenger and guide. Now she seems comfortable in that role, crossing thresholds with ease and acting very much at home in the dream space. She sets the dream's action in motion and introduces new images, showing the other dream figures how to play, move, drive, and even kiss. She greets Michael, arranges a meeting between him and his mother, and introduces him to me. Finally, she guides us down tree-lined streets and seems to take great pleasure in the ride. Her mediating energy moves us into, through, and out of various locations and levels of experience. It is the catalyzing agent that "drives" the dream to its surprising conclusion.

The symbol of the kiss occurs twice in this dream and invites further exploration. As Jungian analyst Marilyn Marshall observes in her article "A 'Close-up' of the Kiss," kisses come in many flavors and express a variety of moods.[10] There are kisses of union, possession, affection, courage, betrayal, and erotic love, to mention just a few. Some kisses fill us with divine energy, and some, like the kisses of the Dementors in the Harry Potter books, suck the very soul out of us. Marshall points out that the Latin word for "kissing" (osculatio), is closely related to the word for "mouth" (*ostium*), which "includes as part of its meaning 'door, entrance.'"[11] Thus the kiss represents "an opening, an entrance to another realm,… [a] quality of union with, or assimilation of, an aspect of the Other."[12]

In my dream, both kisses are gestures of greeting and affection. When Elizabeth kisses Michael, it is as though she is saying hello to an old friend. He comes from the other side of the fence, as though he has been there all along but has just discovered that she is living next door. When they kiss at the boundary between their worlds, an exchange of energy occurs. He is the only male figure in the dream and represents an infusion of masculine energy into a feminine world. In "real life," as his mother had told me, he possessed keen intelligence, a lively spirit of adventure, and a finely tuned sense of humor. As he kisses Elizabeth, these qualities enter the dream world with him. After the kiss, he comes into the house and has a brief meeting with his mother. I worry about her reaction, but she does not seem to realize that he is dead and is visiting her in a dream. She had told me that in actual life he would often drop in for quick, unannounced visits; she had also indicated that she did not believe in the afterlife. Now she reacts as though this is one of his regular visits, not a visitation from the "other side." Interpreted subjectively, her image could represent my own skepticism about the afterlife. To this day, my skeptical streak reminds me that we have no way of knowing where dreams of the dead originate. All we can say for certain is that they happen, that they shape and guide our experience of mourning, and that they assist us in coming to terms with the death of our loved ones and finding our way into life again.

In the next scene of the dream, the focus shifts to the image of the old patched-together car that Elizabeth finds on the side of the street. I associated the car to an old jalopy that she won as a booby prize at a stock-car race one summer. Her friend Chris Slay, who made the driftwood memorial mentioned in Chapter 8, was with her at the time and helped her drive the car home. She loved that car, but had no idea what to do with it and no money to pay for the extensive repairs it needed. Eventually she sold it, but she loved to tell the story of her unexpected good luck. In the dream she is just as delighted to find the patchwork car, which seems to be put together using the parts of rusty old heaps. Like the whimsical creatures she makes from the plastic balls, it is a new creation fashioned from cast-off scraps. Common sense says that it should not work, but somehow it does run in the imaginal world. Unlike the car that ran out of gas on Elizabeth and Michael's weekend jaunt, this vehicle does not break down. To my great surprise it starts up, runs smoothly, and becomes our means of transport in the bubble of the dream world. Like a transitional object, it is both found and created, and possesses its own autonomous energy.

As I play with the image of the car, it occurs to me that it is an example of exactly what symbols are, do, and mean in the life of the psyche. New symbols appear when the reconciling and unifying power of the transcendent function is activated. They are at the right place at the right time, and patch many parts together into a cohesive whole. Unifying symbols are unusual and surprising, although they are not always beautiful. They vibrate with psychic energy as they fulfill their bridging and healing function. They most definitely are not created by the ego. Even when they take curious and bizarre form, like the old car, they embody and mediate the numinous power of the Self.

In the next scene of the dream, Elizabeth jumps into the car with a joyful grin and pretends to drive, like a child who is not quite tall enough to reach the pedals. But Michael, who loved to go on road trips, is the one who actually takes the wheel. His active masculine energy drives the car now, while I sit in the passenger seat and Elizabeth is content to take a back seat and enjoy the ride. As we motor along, I feel as though I am in my home town, driving down wide streets with towering elms arching above. Then I notice that the trees are not elms but ginkgoes, and that their fan-shaped leaves are just beginning to turn bright yellow. I say to Elizabeth several times, "Oh, look, the ginkgoes are turning!" This time *I* have something to show *her*, and I don't want her to overlook the beauty of the golden leaves.

Trees, with their roots delving deep into the earth and their branches reaching for the sky, are natural symbols of the connection between heaven and earth. Deciduous trees, such as the elm and the ginkgo, which annually shed and regenerate their leaves, are "above all symbols of the rebirth of life, victorious over death."[13] In my Midwestern home, Dutch elm disease wiped out most of the elms in the late 1960s. But on a recent trip I noticed that a few hardy specimens had survived as reminders of the tall green arches that once graced the streets. The ginkgo, too, is a survivor, "the oldest surviving species of tree known to exist, with a botanical history spanning more than 200 million years." For centuries it "has served as a symbol of hope and peace in its native land of China." In 1945, six ginkgoes survived the atomic destruction of Hiroshima. It is also regarded in Eastern cultures as a symbol of duality, "the importance of both the yin and the yang."[14] Many ginkgoes thrive in the small southern city where I live today, some planted along roadsides and two magnificent specimens gracing the local cemetery.

In the Georgia town where Elizabeth grew up, gingko trees line the main street and a "Golden Ginkgo Jamboree" is held each fall. One year she bought a gold-dipped ginkgo leaf pendant at the festival and gave it to me as a present. So, in addition to its significance as an ancient form of life, the ginkgo represents to me the gift of connection that continues after death. Like that relationship, it grows slowly and must be tended for years before it reaches maturity. But careful attention is rewarded with a tall, hardy tree whose green leaves turn brilliant yellow in the fall, drop in a shower of gold, and bud again in the spring. In my dream, the change from green to gold is just beginning, as if to signify that the cycle of life and death is completing its annual round. The gleam of gold beneath Elizabeth's black hair in my dream of the underworld symbolized the emergence of new consciousness from the *nigredo* of the compost heap. Now the appearance of the golden ginkgo trees signifies that like the cycle of the seasons, the transformation of consciousness continues to unfold.

The enlargement of consciousness is also enhanced by the dream ego's encounter with Michael, who "drives" the action of the next episode of the dream. At first I am anxious about his driving, as though I am afraid that he is not paying enough attention. When a truck approaches from the opposite direction, I reflexively yell at him to watch where he's going. My knee-jerk reaction suggests that I have not quite grasped that things operate differently in the dream world. The rules are not the same here as in the world of waking reality. People appear out of nowhere, create improbable playthings, and drive around in crazy-quilt cars. Dream time flows back and forth between decades, as though the clock runs differently here. The same is true of space: the dreamer is transported from a house to a car, or from the Midwest to the South, in the twinkling of an eye. Trees can be both green and yellow, elm and ginkgo, dead and alive, with no apparent contradiction. The dream figures of Michael and Elizabeth seem to be at home in this alternate universe, but I am not, and in my anxiety I dread a recurrence of the accident that took their lives. But this is not another "replay-of-the-accident" dream. In this dream universe, the accident does not happen. Disaster is averted because there is plenty of room on the road for the car and the truck to pass each other safely. Instead of colliding, the opposites meet, pass, and travel on their respective ways. In the instant of their passing, I feel a perceptible easing of tension. I suddenly realize that this is not an "either/or" universe. Here it is possible to relax, sit back, and enjoy the world as it is.

At this point in the dream, the opposites of parent and child, feminine and masculine, living and "dead" (although he seems very much alive) touch as Michael turns and kisses me on the lips. In that moment, I receive a bit of his bold, adventurous spirit, and perhaps he absorbs a touch of maternal energy from me. But our kiss initiates another change as well: I fall silent and he begins to speak. Perhaps the maternal kiss reminds him of his parents, for he says quite wistfully that he wishes he could visit them and knows that they miss him a lot. Considering that earlier in the dream he had a brief visit with his mother, this wish comes as something of a surprise. He seems to be hoping for another sort of meeting, one that will convince his parents that he is "alive" in another dimension. He seems to want to say to them, "I am here. You are not making me up. I long to touch you, play with you, kiss you. Don't shut me out. Open your minds and hearts and let me in."

But where will this meeting take place? The answer is almost too simple. Before I can think of it myself, Elizabeth pipes up from the back seat and exclaims, "Oh, but you can! You can visit them in their dreams!" She speaks with conviction, but with a wink at me to let me know that this is our little joke: she has been visiting me in my dreams for some time now. She and I both know that our relationship has continued to grow and thrive in these dream visits. This visit is only one of many. Like our drive in the car, it is a journey through a symbolic landscape, full of wonders and yet as real in its own right as a journey in the "real world." As long as we maintain the willing suspension of disbelief, the dream world will be able to hold and contain us.

As soon as she says this, however, the bubble bursts, the dream ends, and I wake up. It seems that our contact in the imaginal world can be maintained only as long as we do not mention it. It is important to be conscious of it, but the knowledge must remain an inner knowing, like the transformation that takes place in the alchemical vessel. Why, then, does Elizabeth pop the bubble? My feeling is that she knows exactly what she is doing when she hints that she has been visiting me in my dreams. She knows that our encounters in the world of dreams must sooner or later come to an end. When the dream is over, the dreamer must return to the waking world and its everyday concerns.

But there is one more episode to come in the form of an epilogue to the dream. As I floated between sleep and waking, the image of a ferryboat drifted into my mind. In many religious traditions, boats represent "the crossing from the realm of the living to the realm of the dead or vice versa. In Greek mythology the ferryman Charon transports the dead in his boat over the boundary river... into the under-world."[15] In ancient Egyptian iconography, images of boats are found in the *Amduat* (a funerary text) and in the tombs of the pharaohs.[16] In these images, the barque of the Sun god carries the dead pharaoh's soul through the netherworld every night so that he may rise again each morning. Thus the boat is another symbol of the mediating energy that links the living and the dead, the upper and lower worlds. I did not want my dream visit with Elizabeth to end, but as the ferryboat appeared, I realized that a turning point had arrived. In my premonitory dream, Elizabeth had vanished into thin air with the magical horses. I could not follow her into the next world, but in the vessel of the imaginal ferryboat she could "cross the great water" and visit me in my dreams.[17] Although separated by death, we could meet in the liminal world that Jung called the objective psyche, Winnicott called the "realm of illusion," and ancient people called the underworld. This insight brought sadness because it emphasized that Elizabeth and I would not meet again in the waking world. But it also brought the consolation that in the imaginal world of dreams, it was possible for us to meet, talk, and play again.

In dreams such as this one, the messengers of the gods appear just as suddenly and unexpectedly as they did in Homer's time. They can take many forms: a guide to the underworld, a young man or woman in the bloom of youth, a play-space equipped with a pile of colorful plastic balls, a junkyard car that shouldn't run (but does), an imaginal ferryboat. They cross the barriers of time and space and conduct us into a realm in which Persephone is both lost and found, Demeter perpetually grieves and rejoices, and life eternally disappears into the earth and dies, only to be born again. When we experience that world ourselves, we begin to understand Jung's words that "the dream, this fleeting and insignificant-looking product of the psyche," is "a harbinger of fate, a portent and comforter, a messenger of the gods."[18] The next chapter examines dreams in which images of the dead offer messages, instructions, and gifts to the living. But first it describes Persephone's return to earth and her joyful reunion with her mother.

Notes

1 See C. G. Jung, *Memories*, 367.
2 For the history of the gods and their relationships, I am indebted to R. Graves, *The Greek Myths*, Vol. 1.
3 C. G. Jung, *Memories*, 417.
4 See Homer, "Hymn to Hermes," in *Homeric Hymns*, 43–64.
5 C. G. Jung, *Psychological Types*, CW 6, § 828.
6 New Oxford American Dictionary, computer application.
7 D. W. Winnicott, "Transitional Objects and Transitional Phenomena," in *Playing and Reality*, 2.
8 *Ibid.*, 13.
9 The Romantic poet Samuel Taylor Coleridge coined this phrase in *Biographia Literaria* (1817) to refer to "that willing suspension of disbelief for the moment, which constitutes poetic faith." See <https://en.wikipedia.org/wiki/Suspension_of_disbelief>
10 M. Marshall, "A 'Close-Up' of the Kiss," 118–132.
11 *Ibid.*, 120.
12 *Ibid.*, 121.
13 *The Herder Symbol Dictionary*, trans. B. Matthews, 202.
14 K. Maier, *The Symbolic Meaning of the Ginkgo Tree*.
15 *The Herder Symbol Dictionary*, trans. B. Matthews, 26.
16 T. Abt and E. Hornung, *Knowledge for the Afterlife: The Egyptian* Amduat—*a Quest for Immortality*.
17 The phrase "to cross the great water" appears often in the *I Ching, or Book of Changes*, trans. R. Wilhelm, English trans. C. F. Baynes.
18 C. G. Jung, *Two Essays on Analytical Psychology*, CW 7, § 21.

Chapter 11

The food of the deep

The pomegranate seed

As Persephone alights from Hermes's chariot, Demeter enfolds her in a joyful embrace. But then she asks if her daughter has eaten anything in the underworld, and Persephone confesses that Hades had fed her a single pomegranate seed, assuring that she would have to return to him for part of every year. No longer a maiden, she cannot return to the innocence of childhood. By eating the pomegranate seed, she has incorporated a bit of the underworld into herself. In psychological terms, her act might represent the loss of a naive attitude to life and a new awareness of the reality of suffering and death.

Ironically, the pomegranate is also a symbol of fertility. In ancient Greece it was sacred to Aphrodite, Demeter, and Hera, the goddesses associated with love, motherhood, and marriage. Newly married Roman women wore wreaths of pomegranate branches in their hair. "In India the juice of the pomegranate was considered to be a remedy for infertility. Opening the pomegranate [was] sometimes seen symbolically as deflowering."[1] Its many seeds denote the abundance of life and its bright red juice resembles life's blood. In the Homeric Hymn, the pomegranate seed may represent the new life growing in Persephone's womb. Pregnancy is not mentioned in the myth, but the Eleusinian Mysteries, which commemorated the myth, incorporated into their ritual the birth of a divine child.[2] Thus the tiny pomegranate seed represents new life which is conceived in the underworld and born after Persephone returns to earth and ascends to Olympus.

The food of the deep

But how does the life of the underworld reveal itself to us today? More specifically, how does it nourish the souls of those who mourn? Soul-nourishment can take the form of gratitude for our loved ones' lives, or even an uncanny sense of their continuing presence. But often it appears in dreams in which they offer us unexpected messages and gifts. In the following dream, which occurred five months after her death and near the date of her birthday, Elizabeth offered me the gift of a fish:

I'm at the beach with Elizabeth. She is swimming around in the water like a mermaid, very much at home and in her element. She catches a fish, swims to the shore and gives it to me. It is still alive and is moving faintly. It is beautiful, with shiny iridescent rainbow colors. I want to throw it back into the water, but somehow I know that Elizabeth wants me to kill it, cook it, and eat it. I hesitate, unable to decide what to do.

I let the fish slip back into the water and hope that it will swim away, but Elizabeth swims after it, catches it, and brings it back to me. I notice that in the process of catching it, her throat has been cut—but she is not in pain, not bleeding, and seems to be all right. She doesn't speak (perhaps she can't), but she has a look of exasperation on her face. I feel that if she could talk, she would say something like, "Mom, this fish is for you and you are meant to have it. It's time for you to get over your squeamishness and go ahead and kill it and eat it. If you don't take it this time, I'll just keep bringing it back until you do!"

In my premonitory dream, which also began at the beach with Elizabeth, she vanished into the sea with the horses. Now she emerges *from* the sea, bringing me a fish she has caught. She presents it to me as though it is sacred food, and conveys without words that I am to kill it, clean it, cook it, and eat it. What is the meaning of this gift, and why is Elizabeth so insistent in offering it to me? Several months later, to honor the dream, I decided to write a paper on the meaning of the fish symbol. I discovered that it is an ancient one, found worldwide in many cultures and religious traditions. In Christianity, Jesus summoned his disciples to become "fishers of men" (Luke 5:1–11), fed the five thousand with five loaves and two fishes (Matt. 14:15–21), and appeared to his disciples after his resurrection, inviting them to share a meal of bread and fish with him (John 21:1–14).[3] Early in the Christian era, the symbol of the fish came to represent Christ, since the letters of the Greek word for "fish," *ichthus*, form an acronym for "Iesous Christos, Theou Huios, Soter" (Jesus Christ, Son of God, Savior).[4] As Christianity spread through the Roman Empire, the image of the fish began to appear on gravestones, urns, and other funerary objects as a symbol of Christ's resurrection from the dead. Today it is seen on jewelry, plaques, and even bumper stickers as an emblem of the Christian faith. As noted in Chapter 6, two of Jung's dreams of his dead father, a Christian pastor, incorporate fish imagery. In his work on the fish symbol, Jung observed that the birth of Christ coincided with the beginning of the astrological age of Pisces, the emblem of which is two fish arranged head to tail. The fish also appears in alchemical texts as an image of "the *prima materia* from which the miraculous birth ensues."[5] The "miraculous birth" refers to the emergence of a new symbol that reconciles previously contradictory opposites.

I also learned that centuries before the Christian era, sacred fish were associated with fertility goddesses and were found in graves and burial grounds. For example, in the mid-1960s, fifteen sandstone sculptures "twice as large as a human head and carved of naturally egg-shaped river boulders" were unearthed at Lepenski Vir, an ancient fishing village in what was then Yugoslavia.[6] These 8,000-year-old sculptures depict creatures with half-fish, half-human features, including triangles and chevrons denoting female genitals. In her book *The Language of the Goddess*, archaeologist Marija Gimbutas suggests that the sculptures represent a fish goddess, "the Mistress of Life and Death, a generative womb."[7] According to her research, the representation of life-giving energy in the form of a fish is found in religious traditions throughout the world. Fish and spiral patterns "asserting rising life power at the moment of death" appear on a Minoan sarcophagus from 1100 BCE.[8] A Boeotian amphora from 700–675 BCE features elaborate decorations incorporating the image of the goddess with a fish in her womb, surrounded by many birds and animals.[9] This image recalls Erich Neumann's description of the Great Goddess: "To her belong all waters, streams, fountains, ponds, and springs, as well as the rain. She is the ocean of life with its life- and death-bringing seasons, and life is her child, a fish eternally swimming inside her."[10] In ancient Syria the fertility goddess Atargatis and her consort Oannes were portrayed in half-human, half-fish form;[11] in classical Greece and Rome the fish was associated with Aphrodite, the goddess of erotic love, and fish were viewed as "aphrodisiac" food.[12]

By bringing me the fish, Elizabeth is asking me to integrate into consciousness these many levels of meaning, from the pre-Christian source of feminine fertility to the Christian symbol of resurrection. She is inviting me to assimilate an archetypal image that represents the eternal cycle of life and death. I (the dream ego) am reluctant to accept her gift because I admire the fish's beauty and don't want to kill it. And so I let it slip back into the water, hoping that I won't have to go through the messy business of gutting and cleaning it. I return the fish to the waters of the unconscious, which must mean that on some level I prefer to remain unconscious myself. But Elizabeth swims out, catches the fish, and brings it back to me, silently communicating that she will keep on doing so until I accept it. Her persistence indicates that there comes a time when the unconscious will not leave us alone until we integrate its contents into our conscious attitude.

Elizabeth appears in this dream in mermaid form, at home in the water as though she were a fish herself. As half-human, half-fishlike creatures, mermaids are portrayed in myth and folklore as messengers between the depths of the unconscious (the sea) and the mundane world of consciousness (the land). The message she brings, in the form of the fish, invites me to assimilate the messier aspects of life, even when that means killing the fish so that I can incorporate its symbolic meaning into myself. Another messy image occurs when she swims out to retrieve the fish and returns with her throat cut. The dream does not reveal how she gets the wound, which prevents her from speaking and forces her to communicate by means of facial expressions and physical gestures. Even so she makes it

Figure 11.1 Pietà
Drawing by Nancy Carter, 1994.

very clear that I must integrate what the fish represents, although that means that I must be a "cutthroat" and take its life.

Many years after this dream, my friend Nancy Carter, an artist who often paints images from her dreams, gave me a drawing entitled *Pietà*, reproduced in Figure 11.1. The image resembles traditional images of Mary holding the dead body of Christ, but here the sorrowing woman holds a fish instead. Like Elizabeth in my dream, she seems to be offering it up as sacrificial food. Pietà images, which recall images of Mary cradling her newborn son in her arms, convey the essence of what Charlotte Mathes terms "mother grief." These archetypal images of joy and sorrow remind us that birth and death are linked in one eternal round. Like Charlotte Mathes and Julie Nicholson, mentioned in Chapter 8, I found comfort in images of the Pietà. I was deeply touched by Nancy's soulful rendition of it, which closely resembled the image in my dream.

In his writings, Jung often interprets the dream image of the fish as a symbol of *any* content that arises from the depths of the unconscious. For example, he recounts the dream of a young woman which begins with her standing on the bank of a river throwing pages of her notes into the water. Then, in her words:

> I had a fishing-rod in my hand. I sat down on a rock and started fishing. Still I saw nothing but water, earth, and rock. Suddenly a big fish bit. He had a silver belly and a golden back. As I drew him to land, the whole landscape became alive: the rock emerged like the primeval foundation of the earth, grass and flowers sprang up, and the bushes expanded into a great forest. A gust of wind blew and set everything in motion.[13]

According to Jung, this young woman had a positive relationship to her unconscious and had dreamed of fish from an early age. Her dream ego sets the dream's action in motion by sacrificing her intellectual written work, sitting down on a rock, and casting her line into the water. When the big fish bites, her patience is rewarded. Jung interprets the silver and gold fish as a symbol of the reconciliation of opposites. The magical animation of the landscape suggests that a profound transformation of personality is taking place. After the gust of wind, which represents powerful spiritual energy, a Wise Old Man figure stands behind the dreamer and says, "The patient ones in the innermost realm are given the fish, the food of the deep."[14] As one of the "patient ones," the dreamer is given spiritual food to nourish her soul.

Individuation after death

My dream of Elizabeth and the fish suggests that the dead continue evolve psychologically and wish to share their newfound wisdom with the living. In *Memories*, Jung cites two dreams of his wife Emma, who had died in 1955, that seem to corroborate this idea. About a year after her death, he dreamed that he had spent a day with her in the south of France. She was engaged on her study of the Grail, which she had not completed before she died. At first he interpreted his dream subjectively, as though it had to do with unfinished work still to be completed by his anima. That analysis yielded nothing new, since he was aware that his anima work remained unfinished. But the thought that his wife was continuing to work on her spiritual development "struck me as meaningful and held a measure of reassurance for me," he wrote.[15]

A later dream about Emma Jung suggests that she had attained a level of wisdom superior to Jung's own:

> I saw her in a dream which was like a vision. She stood at some distance from me, looking at me squarely. She was in her prime, perhaps about thirty, and wearing the dress which had been made for her many years before by my cousin the medium... Her expression was neither joyful nor sad, but, rather, objectively wise and understanding... I knew that it was not she, but

a portrait she had made or commissioned for me. It contained the beginning of our relationship, the events of fifty-three years of marriage, and the end of her life also. Face to face with such wholeness one remains speechless, for it can scarcely be comprehended.[16]

Jung offers no interpretation of this dream, but writes that the objectivity he experienced there was "part of a completed individuation."[17] The dream provided him with an image of his wife as she existed in the objective psyche, the realm of images. Not coincidentally, she was wearing the dress made for her by his cousin Helene Preiswerk, the subject of his doctoral dissertation, whose encounters with spirits of the dead he had regarded as hallucinations. Now, more than fifty years later, he interprets this vision of his wife as an objective fact. Of course this dream, which occurred near the end of Jung's life, may also be interpreted as an image of the wholeness attained by his anima, a vision of his own completed individuation.

Other dreams led Jung to consider the opposite point of view, that the souls of the dead "know" only what they knew at the moment of death, and appear in dreams in order to learn from the living. For example, he cites a dream in which he is visiting a friend who had died two weeks earlier. During his lifetime this friend had not been a reflective man, but in the dream he was sitting with his daughter, who had studied in Zürich and was telling her father about psychology. The dream indicated to Jung that his friend was now "required to grasp the reality of his psychic existence, which he had never been capable of doing during his life."[18] Jung does not offer a subjective interpretation of this dream, but if he had, he might have discovered something about what his own daughters had to teach him about psychology, or about their relationship with him. Instead, he assumes that the two dream figures refer to the father and daughter as they actually existed at the time of the dream—one dead, the other living. According to this line of thought, it is possible for the dead to learn something from their survivors. Jung takes the dream to mean that his friend's daughter was assisting her father in his individuation process, which had not interested him while he was alive.

A dream of my own, this time about my mother, reinforces the notion that the dead sometimes need the help of the living to continue their individuation. Many years after her death, I dreamed that my mother was sitting in a chair next to my bed, regarding me with a clear and open gaze. No words were exchanged, but the expression on her face told me that she had come to ask for my forgiveness. There was also an unspoken message that she would not be able to "move on" and join my father (who had died many years before she did) until I had forgiven her. My relationship with my mother had been ambivalent, marked by both positive and negative features. She died when I was in my late twenties, with many of our differences still unresolved. After thinking about my dream for several days, I had an "active imagination" dialogue with her, in which I was finally able to forgive her and ask for her forgiveness as well. This was my first experience of an after-death dream, and it made a lasting impression on me. If the dream could help my mother continue her individuation and join my father, so much the better—but without question, the dream was a healing experience for me.

Jung's discussion of his dreams of his wife and his friend assume that the dream images of the dead represent objective beings continuing their individuation in the afterlife. My dream of my mother and many of my dreams of Elizabeth could similarly be interpreted as evidence that the process of individuation does not end with death. According to this view, whether the dead contact the living to gain further knowledge, or whether they are able to learn and develop on their own, their psychic development continues. On the other hand, a subjective interpretation of these dreams marks the steps in the dreamer's own individuation journey. But how are we to decide which perspective to adopt? A rule of thumb might be to try a subjective interpretation first, relating the dream to issues in the dreamer's psychological development. If such an interpretation makes no sense, or if the dream possesses an exceptionally numinous feeling-tone, an objective or imaginal view might be considered. Of course, an interpretation on many levels might prove meaningful to dreamers who are suffering the pain of bereavement.

Symbolic gifts

Sometimes the "food of the deep" is an everyday object that takes on special meaning in the context of a dream. For example, Verena Kast cites Elena's account of a dream in which her deceased boyfriend, George, gives her two gifts:

> I am waiting for George. He comes and sits down on a bench under a tree. He hands me a sheet of paper on which there is brown writing, but in mirror image. It is the draft for a scientific paper. I hope that I can read it. Apart from this George gives me a rubber band. I look at him somewhat puzzled and ask: "What am I supposed to do with this bequest?" I am angry at my own lack of tact in reminding him of his death. You see, throughout the dream I am aware that we have buried him. But I also see that he is very much alive.[19]

This dream came a week after George's funeral, while Elena was still trying to accept the reality of his death. The "dead-yet-alive" paradox seen in many bereavement dreams is clearly evident here. Elena even blames herself for her supposed tactlessness in reminding George that he has died, implying that he is not yet aware of that fact himself. (Her conundrum recalls Jung's first dream of his dead father, discussed in Chapter 5, in which Jung castigates himself for thinking that his father is dead.) In her discussion of the dream, Kast notes that Elena was inclined to see the dream figure of George as representing the "real" person, an interpretation that "comforted her a great deal but always plunged her back into mourning."[20] At the same time, she was beginning "to find in [her]self that which had developed in the course of [her] relationship with [George]."[21] Both aspects of the dream's meaning were integral to Elena's eventual healing from the trauma of George's sudden death. She thought of the rubber band as an image of the continuing connection between herself and her beloved. The scientific paper, with its mirror image writing, led her to think of the afterworld as a mirror image of this world, which must be reflected to be understood. The dream implied that the figure of George "would continue to play from the other side of the grave the extraordinarily stimulating role that he had played in [Elena's] life."[22]

My dream of the fish was not the only one in which Elizabeth brought me a symbolic gift. In a brief dream two months later, she showed me some small red stones in a circular container and asked me to select some to be made into a ring. Here the color red, which reminded me of the spot of blood on the sand in my premonitory dream, the red sweater in my dream of tears, and the red seeds and juice of the pomegranate, appeared in a new form. In alchemy, red denotes the appearance of fully embodied consciousness in the individuation process. In his work on alchemical symbolism, E. F. Edinger notes that images of earthly matter (such as the red stones) refer to the operation of *coagulatio*, in which "a psychic content... has become concretized in a particular localized form; that is, it has become attached to an ego."[23] In this process, "[m]oods and affects... coagulate into something visible and tangible; then we can relate to them objectively."[24] With this in mind, I think of the red stones as the crystallization of the wide range of emotions associated with mourning. The circular container and the ring repeat the motif of the eternal round of life and death. The stones may also be interpreted as fragments of the Philosopher's Stone, the goal of the alchemical *opus*. When it appeared in the alchemical vessel, the Red Stone was thought to embody the union of gold and silver, Sun and Moon, the masculine and feminine principles. It referred to the marriage of previously incompatible opposites and the promise of psychological wholeness.

This dream occurred only seven months after Elizabeth's death, at a time when I was not aware that the red stones might refer to alchemical transformation. When Elizabeth offered them to me, she was inviting me to consider their possible meaning, just as she had invited me to explore the symbolic meaning of the fish. In fact, many of my grief dreams invited me to consider a symbol more closely, or to examine and modify an unbalanced, one-sided attitude. If I was anxious, hesitant, or indecisive, the unconscious supported a more courageous and active stance. During the season of active mourning, my dreams consistently supported experiencing the gamut of emotion associated with grief, including sorrow, shock, anger, and horror at the reality of bodily decomposition. Above all, the dreams invited me to explore and play with images—especially the evolving image of Elizabeth. It soon became clear that her dream image was more than a mere memory trace. In the dream world it had a life of its own and increasingly functioned independently of my emotional state, whatever that might be. By offering me the fish and the red stones, she was demonstrating that mourning was a creative process from which something of value and beauty might emerge.

A brief dream from the same period employed the theme of birth to suggest the emergence of new life:

> I'm pregnant with Elizabeth and she is going to be born today. Her father is skeptical, but I insist that we have to hurry if we are going to get to the hospital in time.

Even in the dream, I knew that the baby to be born was an imaginal, not a literal one, conceived in the underworld of the unconscious like Persephone's child, and brought to birth in the realm of the imagination. Here the dream ego insists that an imaginal child is about to be born, while the dream father (who is a scientist in "real life") represents a more skeptical, rationally oriented attitude. The tension between the two attitudes—the "believing" and the doubtful—runs throughout my grief dreams, but here the dream ego's certainty overrides the dream father's skepticism.

Another dream came soon after the first anniversary of Elizabeth's death, while I was on an Easter holiday in a small Swiss village. On Easter Eve I dreamed,

> Elizabeth's face is painted in a red and blue spiral design, as in the "face-winding game" we used to play together. Her nose is red and from it a red line spirals out until it reaches the circumference of her face. The space between the red lines is bright blue.

On Easter Eve, the Christian Church observes the Great Vigil to commemorate Christ's descent into Hell to redeem the souls of those who had died before him. This night is a thin time during which the faithful await His emergence from the grave as the Risen Christ. The image of the spiral, an ancient symbol of cyclical return and renewal, is "connected with the idea of death and rebirth: entering the mysterious earth womb, penetrating to its core, and passing out again by the same route."[25] In association to the image, I remembered a "face-winding game" that Elizabeth and I used to play as part of her childhood bedtime ritual. As she lay on her back, I would place my index finger lightly on her nose, then slowly wind it outwards in a clockwise spiral until I reached a point at the top of her forehead. Then I would "unwind" the spiral by moving my finger back in a counterclockwise direction, until I reached her nose again. Often she would ask me to repeat the ritual several times before she fell asleep. At the time I had no idea that the spiral was an ancient symbol of death and rebirth. But through its appearance in my dream, it became "concretized in a particular localized form" and invited an archetypal interpretation.

The dream spiral is red and blue, two primary colors that evoke two polar opposites. Red, the warm color of blood and passion, is associated with the masculine principle, movement, and activity. Blue, the cool color of the sky and the sea, is associated with heaven, water, purity, and the feminine principle. In my dream the spiral holds the two colors and their contrasting energies in a finely tuned balance of movement and stillness, action and tranquility. In this archetypal image, the opposites move and rest together in an eternal dance. I woke up thinking that I would like to paint this image, and several months later I dreamed:

I am photocopying Elizabeth's self-portrait photograph so that I can paint the red and blue spiral on it. There are other photographs of her too. Some are familiar, but there are also some new ones.

As part of a school photography project, Elizabeth had created a self-portrait by placing a mirror on the floor, pouring water on it, and taking a black-and-white picture of her reflection. At first glance, the portrait seems to be an abstract study in shades of black, white, and gray. But upon closer inspection, her face becomes visible through what appears to be a rain-spattered window. Her eyes

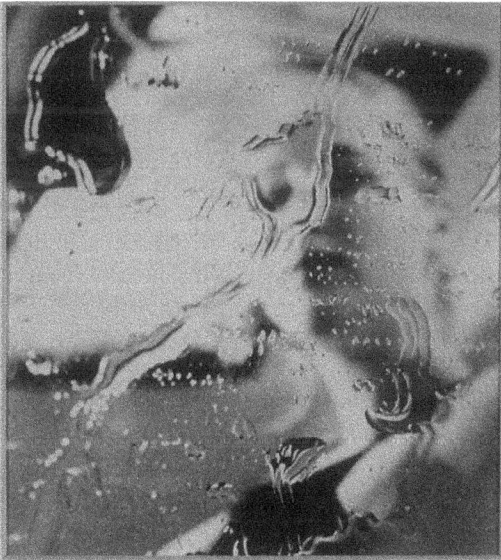

Figure 11.2 Self-portrait
Photograph by Elizabeth Wood, 1987.

regard the viewer from a great distance, with a look of detachment. The sense of seeing (and being seen by) someone from the world "behind the looking glass" is quite uncanny. In my dream, the process of photocopying the image establishes another degree of separation between it and the viewer. The final effect is that the image of Elizabeth's face recedes ever further into the distance. The mirror, the water, the reflection, the photograph, the photocopy: all render her image ever more inaccessible. Painting the red and blue spiral on the image (something I tried to do, with limited success) may have represented my attempt to "fix" it in my memory, to introduce life and color into a shadowy, monochromatic picture. But from another perspective, painting the red and blue spiral on the black-and-white photograph brings memory, emotion, imagination, and archetypal meaning together in a complex but balanced whole.

As this dream ended, I had the sense that other photographs—some old, some new—were lying on a nearby table. I took this to mean that while familiar images of Elizabeth would linger in my memory, others would be added to the collection. In fact, all of my grief dreams included new images that enhanced my appreciation for what Jung called "the potentialities and arts of the unconscious."[26] The images challenged me to take them in, work with them, play with them, digest them. I felt that if I could do this, I could feed my psyche with the food of the deep. In other words, I could accept the symbolic fish that Elizabeth had offered me, rather than throwing it back into the water. That image stays with me whenever I am confronted with a troubling, perplexing, or frightening dream. There is nourishment to be found in the dream, if I am willing to do the work required to convert the raw material into edible food.

This chapter has focused on accepting and assimilating the images, gifts, and messages offered by the dead in grief dreams. Whatever we believe about the afterlife and individuation after death, individuation continues for the living and working with dreams is very much a part of the process. In mourning, however, there comes a time when the dream images of the dead take their leave of us. Sometimes they bless us as they depart, but often they simply say goodbye and go. There is a feeling-tone of finality about these dreams, a sense that the images of the dead have done their work and are needed no more. The next chapter takes up the subject of farewell dreams and the completion of the cycle of mourning.

Notes

1 *The Herder Symbol Dictionary*, trans. B. Matthews, 152.
2 C. G. Jung and C. Kerényi, *Essays on a Science of Mythology*, 142–144.
3 *The Holy Bible*, King James Version.
4 *The Herder Symbol Dictionary*, trans. B. Matthews, 77.
5 C. G. Jung, *Aion*, *CW* 9ii, § 245.
6 M. Gimbutas, *The Language of the Goddess*, 260.
7 *Ibid.*
8 *Ibid.*, 263.

 9 *Ibid.*, 259.
10 E. Neumann, *The Great Mother,* 222.
11 M. Esther Harding, *Woman's Mysteries: Ancient and Modern, 162.*
12 B. Walker, *The Woman's Dictionary of Symbols and Sacred Objects*, 374.
13 C. G. Jung, *Aion, CW* 9ii, § 236.
14 *Ibid.*
15 C. G. Jung, *Memories*, 340–341.
16 *Ibid.*, 327.
17 *Ibid.*, 339.
18 *Ibid.*, 340.
19 V. Kast, *A Time to Mourn: Growing through the Grief Process*, 35.
20 *Ibid.,* 36.
21 *Ibid.*
22 *Ibid.*, 35.
23 E. F. Edinger, *Anatomy of the Psyche*, 83.
24 *Ibid.*, 100.
25 B. Walker, *The Woman's Dictionary of Symbols and Sacred Objects*, 14.
26 C. G. Jung, *Memories*, 335.

Chapter 12

"I have a gift for you"

Parting gifts

At the end of Homer's "Hymn to Demeter," the goddess shows humans how to perform the Eleusinian Mysteries, her sacred rites. Those who were initiated into the Mysteries were not permitted to divulge their secrets, so to this day we do not know exactly what took place there. We do know, however, that at the climax of the ritual a single mown ear of corn (wheat or barley) was shown to the initiates, who experienced a "vision of birth as a source from which life, growth, and replenishment spring in inexhaustible plenty."[1] The ear of corn, a symbol of the Kore (Persephone) was Demeter's divine gift to the human race, representing the end of the famine she had brought upon the earth. As a symbol of both individuality and continuity, the ear of corn contained the essence of the ears that had grown before and those that were yet to come. It impressed upon the participants the truth that life and death follow each other in an eternal, unbroken round: that is the myth's enduring reality.

The experience of mourning does not end with a literal reunion or the establishment of sacred rites. But often, dreams of farewell include a gift or blessing that blunts the pain of separation and leaves the dreamer with an enduring symbol of connection. Two years after Elizabeth's death I had a dream in which she left me with two parting gifts:

Several young people are developing photographs. One is a girl who looks like Elizabeth. At first her back is to me, but when she turns around and I see that it is indeed Elizabeth. She is wearing jeans and a simple navy-blue T-shirt, and her hair is cut shorter than it was in life. I am overwhelmed with joy and call out her name. She looks down at me with her wonderful smile and I can see all the features of her face very clearly. We hug and I ask, "How are you?"—but then I feel that this is a silly question because I know that she is dead. She replies, "Well, I'm older." I look more closely and see that this is true: she has matured and looks as though she is about twenty.

This surprises me because I assumed that she had stopped growing when she died.

Then she turns to me and says, "I have a gift for you." I look around and see a small sporty-looking red convertible. Elizabeth seems very happy with it, but is a bit disappointed that I don't immediately recognize it as my "gift." She gets into it and it takes off like a plane, at first taxiing on the ground and then soaring into the air. She turns and waves to me and I wave back, calling "Come back!" But as she flies away, I know that she is gone for good.

At the end of the dream I see that she has left me another gift: three pieces of partially unwrapped chocolate. The message seems to be that she wanted to leave something behind to prove that she was really there—that I wasn't just making the whole thing up.

The first section of this dream repeats the motif of photography, which appeared in a dream discussed in the previous chapter. In that dream Elizabeth's photographic image was receding into the background and becoming ever more distant. But in this dream she is vibrantly present and I can see her features clearly. It is as though this image of her, like Jung's dream vision of his wife, has been created just for me, so that I will never forget the shape of her face and the radiance of her smile. I really do not need to ask, "How are you?" because I can see for myself that she is thriving. I feel silly as I ask the question, because at the same time I know that she is dead. And yet I have to ask, and her answer surprises me: "Well, I'm older." As soon as she says this, I see that it is true. Something about her is different: it is not just her new haircut and new clothes. There is an aura of assurance and peace about her, as though she has matured beyond her years. Perhaps individuation does continue after death. Or perhaps my image of her has also matured, so that she now appears in altered form.

In previous dreams, Elizabeth was trying on or wearing various types of clothing, as though she was searching for just the right outfit to wear in her new state. Sometimes she was wearing a dress from childhood, or her characteristic jeans and baggy T-shirt, or "retro" outfits that looked like they had come from the thrift store. Her hair was also a prominent feature, whether she was combing it with her fingers, covering it up with a black wig, or letting it flow as she did in actual life. In this dream, she is wearing jeans and a simple T-shirt that fit comfortably on her slender body, and her shoulder-length hair falls softly around her face. It appears that she has finally found a simple, easy style that suits her well. If hair symbolizes ideas that grow from the head, and clothing represents the persona, then she seems to have found a natural manner of thinking and self-presentation appropriate to her new level of maturity.

The next dream image is the little red convertible, which she describes as a gift to me. It did not remind me of a car that she, I, or anyone else in our family had ever owned. In fact, I couldn't think of anyone I knew who drove such a car. (Later, Michael's mother told me that it reminded her of a car he had owned—but I did not know this at the time.) Its red color, which represents full-blooded consciousness in the alchemical process, had appeared in many other dreams. But this car—perhaps a vehicle of that new consciousness—could fly! Elizabeth could put the top down, let the wind blow through her hair, and take off into the sky, fired up with the spirit of adventure. And that is exactly what she did, as if to imply that the gift was not the car itself, but the image of her climbing into it, taxiing down the runway, and soaring into the heavens. Even as she waved goodbye and I called, "Come back!" I knew that she had left for good and that I could not go with her.

Like earlier dreams, this one had faint biblical overtones. It reminded me of the stories of the ascension of Elijah, told in II Kings 2:11–12, and of Jesus, described in Acts 1:9–11.[2] I certainly did not think of Elizabeth as a prophet or a savior, and I could almost hear her chuckling about these comparisons. But the associations did come to mind, and I wondered what to make of them. The word "ascension" denotes the act of rising to a higher level in a tree, a building, the atmosphere, or even the hierarchy of being. Devices such as ladders, stairs, elevators, airplanes, and rockets are needed to overcome the force of gravity and accomplish physical ascension. My association to Elijah's chariot, pulled by horses of fire, hearkens back to my initial premonitory dream, in which strange horses lure Elizabeth into the sea. In that dream, she is carried away against her will, but in this dream she departs joyfully, as though she is eager to embark on her new adventure. Her vehicle this time is a sporty red convertible that turns into a magic flying machine. As with the patchwork car in my earlier dream (see Chapter 10), there is something lighthearted and whimsical about this image. The red sports car has a different kind of "horsepower" from the horses in my premonitory dream. Its energy lifts Elizabeth to a new level of being, and in comparison with the car that caused her death, it causes a bittersweet parting rather than a traumatic separation. In the dream I wish that she could stay, but I am not shocked or horrified. Although I am sad to see her go, I know that the time has come.

As soon as she is gone, I see the three pieces of chocolate, partly unwrapped and waiting to be eaten, that she has left behind as a farewell present. She knew about (and shared) my fondness for chocolate, so she was aware that I would enjoy the gift. But until I did a bit of research on the symbolism of chocolate, I was not aware that it has important religious significance in Central and South American cultures. The ancient Aztecs believed that chocolate was a gift from the plumed serpent god Quetzalcoatl, who assumed human form, descended to earth, and presented the human race with a gift from the garden of Paradise: the cacao tree. He showed them how to plant the tree, harvest its fruit, and use the beans to prepare his favorite drink. Linnaeus, the nineteenth-century botanist, memorialized that legend by naming the chocolate tree *Theobroma cacao*, the "Food of the Gods," from the Greek words "theo[s]" (god) and "broma" (food).[3] Elaine Gonzalez, an expert on cooking with chocolate, notes that it plays an important role in Mexican life and in death rituals. The cacao pod was considered the perfect offering to the gods during sacrificial rites, because it symbolized the heart and melted chocolate represented blood. To sustain them on their journey to the afterlife, ancient nobles were buried with cocoa beans to use as payment on arrival. Even today, in remote villages in southern Mexico, a gourd of chocolate is included in every burial to soothe the spirit in its new life. And in Mexico's annual "Day of the Dead" celebrations, mourners present the dead with gifts of chocolate.[4] Thus chocolate functions as a mediating symbol between the divine and the human, heaven and earth, the living and the dead. Like the fish in my earlier dream, Persephone's pomegranate seed, and the single mown ear of corn, it points to the eternal cycle of life and death.

But in my dream, I do not offer chocolate to the gods or place it on Elizabeth's grave to soothe *her* spirit. Instead she leaves it behind in the dream world to comfort *mine*. Like the fish in my earlier dream, it is food—but food of a different sort. Raw cacao beans must be fermented, roasted, peeled, and ground before they can be consumed. Even more processing goes into the making of cocoa and the chocolate confections we enjoy today. The process is not unlike the alchemical *opus*, which undergoes many stages until the Philosopher's Stone, or alchemical gold, is produced. Like the small red stones in my previous dream, it involves the *coagulatio*, or crystallization, of experience into concrete form. Therefore the chocolate that Elizabeth leaves me is not raw material like the fish, but the final product of a long and painstaking process, not unlike individuation or mourning. By implication, she is letting me know that my two-year period of intense grief is coming to a close. The arduous process has produced three pieces of delicious chocolate, unwrapped and ready for me to consume.

After the second anniversary of Elizabeth's death, my vivid dreams of her ended as suddenly as they had begun. I missed them, just as I missed her, but I was grateful for the consolation and guidance they had provided during that painful time. Years later, when I began to gather and study bereavement dreams, I learned that the motif of a farewell gift or visit appears quite often in the dreams of the bereaved. The rest of this chapter is devoted to other dreams in which the theme of farewell appears.

A tip of the hat

In his thesis, "The Alchemy of Death," Emmanuel Kennedy discusses many dreams collected through correspondence and personal contact with the bereaved. He notes that in many "metapsychic" dreams, the figure of the deceased disappears into a dark place such as a forest, the sea, an abyss, or (as in the case of the following dream) a large ship. Four months after her father's death, a woman dreamed:

> My mother and I walked down a long boardwalk with my father. At a certain juncture, we stopped and my father continued on down the boardwalk. He finally reached a very large ship which was tied up and waiting at the

end of the dock. He turned to us and tipped his beret in farewell. He then entered the big ship which was very dark against a deep midnight blue sky. On awaking I felt that my father was safe, going on a new journey, and courteous as usual with his gesture of farewell.[5]

In this dream, the dreamer and her parents walk together down a boardwalk, a symbol of the transitional space between land and sea. At a certain point, she and her mother know that they can go no further, while the father figure walks on until he reaches the ship that will carry him out to sea on his new journey. Before he embarks, however, he courteously tips his beret to the dreamer and her mother in a gesture of farewell. He seems to be reassuring them that all will be well on his voyage. In the context of the dream, his gesture conveys his message without words.

In many spiritual traditions, ships are regarded as symbolic vessels which ferry the souls of the dead into the next world. For example, in the Egyptian *Amduat*, the barque of the Sun god, Re, transports him "through the darkness of the night to his own rebirth in the morning."[6] In Greek mythology, "the ferryman Charon transports the dead in his boat over the boundary river into the underworld."[7] In our own time, J. R. R. Tolkien's modern-day myth, *The Lord of the Rings*, ends with Frodo's departure from Middle-earth in a great white ship. Before he embarks, he says a final goodbye to his three hobbit friends and gives Sam, without whom his quest to destroy the Ring would have failed, the book he has written about their adventures. His parting gift guarantees that the story of the Ring will continue to be told long after he is gone. It is not clear from the text whether Frodo's departure signifies his death, but like the dream father who tips his hat, he is at peace and is ready to begin his final journey.[8]

"I can see the stars"

A novel by contemporary author Robert Hellenga, *The Fall of a Sparrow,* is the story of a classics professor named Woody, whose twenty-two-year-old daughter, Cookie, is killed in a terrorist bombing in Italy. (The novel is based on the actual bombing of the train station in Bologna in 1980, but the events and characters are fictional.) Near the end of the story, Woody has the following dream:

He dreamed... of Cookie. She must have been twelve or thirteen because she was wearing her first pair of glasses and looking up at the sky. It was dark and she was standing out on the back-porch steps... "I can see them perfectly, Pop," she cried; "I can see the stars." And he knew that she had finally come to say good-bye. She ran towards him, and in his eagerness to embrace her he started forward, but she slipped through his arms, like ether, like air, like a dream.[9]

In Woody's dream, Cookie is on the verge of puberty, about to make her transition into womanhood. With her new glasses, perhaps a symbol of new acute vision, she can see the stars—and perhaps even catch a glimpse of eternity. But before she leaves, she comes to say the goodbye she was not able to say in life. She runs to her father, but when he reaches for her, she slips through his arms "like ether, like air, like a dream." As a classics professor, Woody is aware that his dream encounter mirrors the reunion between Odysseus and his mother in *The Odyssey* (discussed in Chapter 8), about which Odysseus says, "Three times she went sifting through my hands, like a shadow, or a dream."[10] Like Odysseus, to whom he often compares himself, Woody journeys to the underworld of grief in the aftermath of Cookie's death. As he slowly and painfully learns to live without her, he also learns to hold in his heart the image of her young and whole and running towards the stars. And just as Odysseus returns from Hades with a new orientation to life, Woody awakens from this dream and resumes his life with the "quiet revelation" that "death need not poison life."[11]

Packing for a trip

The next example was recounted by a Jungian analyst and colleague, who had an important dream a few days after her mother's death over thirty-five years ago. The dreamer reported that she felt "quite comforted" by the dream and shared it with her sisters on the way to choose their mother's casket:

> I am sitting with my father. We are in a hotel room… seated in two chairs at right angles to each other, in the corner of the room with a table between us. We are the ages we were at that time. We sit and say nothing, but together we watch my mother, who is also in the room. She is probably in her early twenties (she was sixty-three when she died); she is in a navy blue and white polka-dot dress, 1940s style. She looks wonderful—red lipstick and wavy dark hair, shoulder length. She is standing on the other side of a bed, packing a suitcase for a trip. She is clearly excited and happy, busy putting things in the case. She does not seem to notice us or acknowledge our presence. We are clearly observers—not connected with whatever is she is preparing to do.
>
> As she busily packs, I ask her, "Can I go with you?" She does not respond at all, but simply continues her packing. My sense is not that she is intentionally ignoring me, but that she is already beyond me in some way. She finishes her packing, goes to the door of the hotel room, opens it, and on the other side, standing and greeting her, is my twin sister, who died eleven years earlier. She is the age she was when she died. They are very happy to see each other, and again, my father and I are not part of what is happening for them. We sit and watch.

The death of the dreamer's twin sister as a teenager was a major trauma for her family, but now the image of her sister appears at the door, as if to greet her mother and conduct her on the journey for which she has been preparing. As Aniela Jaffé notes, the motif of death as "a journey undertaken by the soul, whose goal we cannot fathom," appears in many grief dreams.[12] The image of a door through which the deceased passes also appears frequently. In this dream, the present, the past, and the time of the mother's young womanhood are compressed into a single timeless moment. The implication seems to be that death, like adolescence and young womanhood, is a time of transition to whatever awaits the mother and daughter on the other side of the open door. As the action of the dream unfolds, the dreamer and her father sit and watch, as though observing a tableau that is being enacted just for them. The mother may or may not be aware of their presence and behaves as if "she is already beyond [us] in some way." When the dreamer asks if she can go along, her mother does not respond or acknowledge the question. Her attention is focused entirely on preparing for her journey. This dream does not include a verbal message, a parting gift, or a final embrace. But to the dreamer, the image of her mother young, well, and reunited with her long-dead daughter was a gift to her and to her family.

A brother's farewell

The next dream comes from my friend Nancy Carter, who created the Pietà drawing seen in Chapter 11. Several years after her brother's death she dreamed:

> The dream of Ben occurred… about a month after David and I began living together. There was a very strong sense of being with Ben, but no sense of where, and he told me that he was going away… There was no conversation about it. I had the feeling that he was turning me over to David's care. He has not appeared in my dreams since. I felt both sad—it seemed like a final severing of our deep connection—and glad that he was free of his ties to the past and could move wholly into his present, whatever that is.

Nancy was close to her brother and grieved deeply when he died, especially since his death was unexpected and occurred in another country under mysterious circumstances. After living alone for many years, she had recently begun living with David, who later became her husband. In the dream, the figure of her brother comes to tell her that he is going away, with the tacit understanding that he knows about her new relationship and is entrusting her to David's care. She has mixed emotions in the dream, which she regarded as both a blessing and a farewell. Her sadness at the "final severing of our deep connection" is tempered by the comforting knowledge that her brother is no longer encumbered by his "ties to the past." On the subjective level, the dream suggests that she, too, has been freed from her own ties to the past and is ready to "move wholly" into her new relationship. As a loving inner figure, Ben presents her with an affirming gift by blessing her relationship to the new man in her life.

A ritual of goodbye

The final example of a farewell dream sets the experience of leave-taking in the archetypal context of a religious ritual. The dreamer is a Jungian analyst and friend whose mother had died six months earlier. This is her dream:

I was arriving at a great stadium. It was like an amphitheater in the square. Down in the middle was an altar with twelve priests or ministers who were going through the Mass or service of Communion. It was a huge place and everything and everyone was in white.

I knew it was about the Great Mother and I knew I was there because my mother had recently died. I had to go down and take Communion before the final ritual, the final goodbye. I made my way down to the front and when I got close, one of the priests recognized that I was one of the ones who had to be served. She came to me, I knelt and she gave me the Communion.

I was escorted out by someone who took me to the back, where there was a white hearse. The person asked me and my sister (who suddenly appeared) if we knew the rules and we said that we did. He/she then restated the importance of knowing that we were about to experience an illusion, not a physical reality. That it was important to remember it was the final goodbye and that we could move only within the boundaries that were given. We were asked if we were ready and we both took deep breaths and indicated "yes."

Then they opened the back of the car and my mother sat up slowly. I knew it was the last time I would see her, would be able to touch and smell and be near her. The power of being in her presence like this was almost overwhelming. She spoke my name. We gently touched each other and hugged. I touched the back of her hand like I used to when I was a child. She, too, knew it was the last goodbye. We were all deeply, deeply sad and grateful to have this chance, this last time together to share our love. Then it was time to go. The dream ended with me reminding myself that it was an illusion and a blessing and that it was time now to let her go.

This memorable dream includes many elements found in other grief dreams: the joy of reunion, the sharing of an embrace, the acceptance of the reality of death, and the sadness of a final parting. The action of the dream occurs in a great stadium, an amphitheater in the square which resembles a mandala. As Jung frequently observed, the mandala, which can take the form of either a circle or a square, is a symbol of wholeness. The square is "a symbol of the combined effects of the four elements and thus of the powers of Aphrodite, Demeter, Hestia, and Hera, subsumed in the mother of the gods, Rhea."[13] In this dream, the stadium is a sacred space dedicated to the Great Mother. The temple priests are both male and female, as in the Eleusinian Mysteries. The color white, prominent in the dream, is the color of purity, initiation, and (in many cultures) mourning. As Edinger notes, white is associated with the *albedo*, or "whitening," phase of the alchemical *opus*, in which the intense affects and desires of the *nigredo* phase are burned away. The residue is "the incorruptible 'glorified body,' which has survived the purifying ordeal," he writes.[14] Taken together, the symbolism of the square, the Communion service, and the priests dressed in white evoke an intense spiritual atmosphere.

The ceremony that takes place in the stadium has to do with the transition from the literal to the imaginal, the personal to the archetypal level of being. The passage from one to the other is so important that a special Communion service is held to prepare the initiates for it. In the Christian service of Holy Communion, literal bread and wine are transformed into the symbolic body and blood of Christ. But even before the time of Christ, pilgrims to Eleusis and other sacred sites ate symbolic spiritual food and drank wine to prepare for their induction into the great mysteries. In this dream, a female priest serves Communion to the dreamer, while another guide stresses that what is about to happen will take place in the realm of "illusion," i.e., the imaginal realm in which the living and the dead are able to meet. After the dream mother sits up in her coffin, she shares a final embrace with her daughters. All three know that this is their last meeting, and feel both sad and grateful. As the dream ends, the dreamer reminds herself that it is now time to let her mother go. But the sorrow of parting is endurable because she, her mother, and her sister are held in the eternal embrace of the Great Mother. My friend commented that her dream was not so much about life after death, as "about life, love, and transition on the unconscious level in addition to that on the ego level." Later she began to study Sophia, the archetypal figure of feminine wisdom, and in that work her connection to the Great Mother continues to nourish her.

The legacy of the dead

This book has traced my personal mourning process as reflected in my dreams following the sudden death of my daughter. I have framed my discussion in the context of the ancient myth of Demeter and Persephone, and have included dreams told by others, selections from myth and literature, references to religious traditions, and passages from the work of C. G. Jung. Since Jung's death in 1961, many analytical psychologists have continued his exploration of the subject of grief dreams. I like to think that he would be interested in what his students have learned about "pre- and post-mortal psychic phenomena," and I hope that my work will contribute to the understanding of this elusive subject. Throughout his life Jung struggled to reconcile his scientific and academic training with his religious background and his own spiritual inclinations. While attempting to maintain his scientific objectivity, he also worked to formulate his own personal "myth" of life after death. As a man of science and also a man of faith, he attempted to hold the tension between the two viewpoints and the two sides of himself. At times, the difficulty of bearing the tension is painfully apparent in his work. While he cautions us to be wary of easy answers to the question of life after death, he also advises us to formulate our own "myth" of the afterlife, based on the hints offered in our dreams. I have sought to maintain his careful balance of skepticism and openness throughout this book.

In the end, our views about life after death are a matter of individual belief. Although I would like to believe in the existence of an afterlife and a reunion with our deceased loved ones, I remain skeptical about these matters. But my dreams of Elizabeth, as well as the dreams and experiences of others, have convinced me that grief dreams can help us heal from even the most devastating losses. No one can be certain whether the spirits of the departed are "really" present in our dreams. But it *is* certain that their vivid images visit us in our dreams and remain with us for the rest of our lives. My dream images of my daughter guided me through the first years of bereavement and left a lasting impression on my psyche. The dreams were so vivid that I could not doubt their authenticity as psychic facts. As the dream series unfolded, Elizabeth became my guide to the underworld of the unconscious and led me to believe in the transformative power of dreams. For her, and for them, I will always be grateful.

Notes

1 C. Kerényi, "Kore," in C. G. Jung and C. Kerényi, *Essays on a Science of Mythology*, 146.
2 *The Holy Bible*, King James version.
3 E. Gonzalez, "In Search of Chocolate: Mexico's Sacred Legacy," on her website, <www.elainegonzalez.com>, 1994.
4 *Ibid.*
5 E. X. Kennedy, "The Alchemy of Death," 58.
6 T. Abt and E. Hornung, *Knowledge for the Afterlife*, 24.
7 *The Herder Symbol Dictionary*, trans. B. Matthews, 26.
8 J. R. R. Tolkien, *The Return of the King,* 1007. In one of his letters, Tolkien indicated that Frodo's voyage did not signify his death, but his passage into "a period of reflection and peace and a gaining of a truer understanding of his position in littleness and in greatness, spent still in Time amid the natural beauty of the Earth unspoiled by evil"—*The Letters of J. R. R. Tolkien*, 328.
9 R. Hellenga, *The Fall of a Sparrow*, 421.
10 *Ibid.*, 422.
11 *Ibid.*, 432.
12 A. Jaffé, *Apparitions*, 43.
13 *The Herder Symbol Dictionary*, trans. B. Matthews, 180.
14 E. F. Edinger, *Anatomy of the Psyche*, 40.

Epilogue

"I have a new name"

After the dream of the red sports car and the gift of chocolate, my dream encounters with Elizabeth came to an end. I hoped that one day I would be able to write about them, but two years after her death I was still not emotionally ready to try. And so I concentrated on finishing my training, moving back to the U.S., and beginning to practice as an analyst. I also began to do some teaching and discovered that I enjoyed the challenge of that work. I kept the journals in which I had recorded my dreams, waiting for the right time to write about them. Then, more than ten years after Elizabeth's death, came one more vivid dream:

I'm flying, floating, or shooting through space in a direction that feels like "down"—but it could be any direction. Elizabeth is there, and I realize that this is another dream encounter with her. I am overjoyed to see her and be with her again.

Then the scene changes and we are walking and talking together. I notice that she is almost thirty—the age that she would be if she had lived. She is lovely and graceful, and is wearing a bit of makeup and a blue dress with a jacket. Her shoulder-length hair falls lightly around her face.

We walk and talk for a long time. I don't remember the details of the conversation, but she tells me that there is much challenging, satisfying work to do in the place where she is now. She is working hard and loving it. I realize that she has more insight than I do, and so I ask her what is next for me. What is my task now? She does not answer in words, but points to a cluster of little white kittens lying on the ground near our feet. Their eyes are barely open and their tiny paws and noses are pink and tender. We walk carefully to avoid stepping on them, and I say, "All the little Ariels!" I get the sense that they are now to be in my care. Elizabeth says matter-of-factly, "They seem to be in a pretty good place."

Then she turns to me and says shyly, "I have a new name." She is proud and happy about this, but wants my blessing and hopes that I won't feel hurt that she no longer uses the name her father and I had given her. I am curious and ask her, "What is it?" She says a word that starts with a "T," in a language that I don't know. I try to pronounce it, but can't quite do it. Then she says shyly but proudly that she has a new title too. Again I can't pronounce it, but I can tell that she is full of joy about it. I blow on my fingernails and polish them on my shirt in a gesture that means, "Good for you! I'm so proud of you!"

Then suddenly she is gone, vanishing into thin air. I want to hold her and prolong the moment, but I know that I can't. I'm laughing and crying and wanting to tell people about what has happened. I see a group of women and exclaim, "She was here! It wasn't a dream, it was a vision!" Then I wake up.

This dream felt like the culmination of all the dreams that had gone before. It had the immediacy and sense of presence of my earlier grief dreams—or even more so. I knew from the outset that Elizabeth was dead and that this was another dream encounter with her. But this time I was not afraid that the "bubble" of the dream world would burst and that she would vanish too soon. Somehow I knew that we would stay together as long as we needed to and that the dream would not end until we had said and done all that we needed to say and do.

The theme of individuation after death recurs in this dream, for Elizabeth appears in it as a mature woman. She seems very comfortable in herself, and her simple dress and natural hairstyle suit her well. Once again, the color blue, symbolic of heaven and the divine, appears in her clothing. But her appearance is only the outward sign of her inner transformation. The profound change becomes clear as she explains the satisfying work she is doing now. My difficulty understanding her recalls Jung's last recorded dream of his father, in which the dream father is explicating an Old Testament passage so rapidly that his son cannot understand him. In both dreams, a long-dead loved one appears as an advanced or enlightened soul. Since the dream implies that Elizabeth has attained a high level of wisdom, I ask her to tell me what is next for me. What is the work that I am meant to do for the rest of my life? Her response is startling, delightful, and totally unexpected. Instead of using words, she points down to the ground, where a cluster of white kittens is lying at our feet. In my first dream reunion with her, she had embraced me and said, "Let your tears fertilize my ground." Now, ten years later, she points to the ground as if to suggest that the "fruit" of my tears is the profusion of kittens that has sprung up around us. Judging from their recently opened eyes, they are only about ten days old. They are small and vulnerable, and their tiny paws and noses are pink and tender. But where is their mother? It seems that I am "it" and that it is my job to take care of them until they are able to fend for themselves. In reality, this task would involve frequent feeding, grooming, and litter-box training. The caretaker of these kittens would have to devote herself to the job for several weeks, with not much time for anything else. But in the dream I feel eager to do it, especially when Elizabeth says that the kittens "seem to be in a pretty good place."

My exclamation "All the little Ariels!" refers to a cat that Elizabeth introduced into our family when she was in high school. Walking home one afternoon, she had met some people who were giving away kittens, among them one little fellow she could not resist. When her brother came to pick me up from work that day, he informed me with a conspiratorial grin that he and his sister had a surprise for me. As soon as we got home they made me sit down, close my eyes, and open my hands on my lap. The moment I felt the soft ball of fur and opened my eyes I was hooked. "Can we keep him until we find him a home?" they pleaded. And then we all burst into laughter. They knew as well as I did that he had found a home and would not be leaving us. We judged that he was only five or six weeks old—too young to be separated from his mother, but old enough to survive with our help. He was pure white, with bright blue eyes and a feisty spirit. He loved to hide under chairs and pounce on anyone foolish enough to walk by. "He thinks our hands and feet are his brothers and sisters," Elizabeth said, and she was right. At the time she was reading *The Tempest* in her English class, and so she named him "Ariel" after the "brave spirit" in Shakespeare's play.[1] The name suited him well, for he was brave, fiery, swift, and ubiquitous. As soon as he learned to climb (and it did not

Figure 13.1 Ariel sitting on the brick wall
Photograph by the author.

take long), he would perch imperially on the roof, in a tree, or on the brick wall at the side of the house, and would not come down until he felt like it.

We soon realized that Ariel was too much of a free spirit to be tamed completely. He had the run of the neighborhood and probably sired many "little Ariels" before we finally had him "fixed." When we went on walks, he would follow us around the block like a dog. He knew what he wanted and almost always got it. And yet he had a tender side as well; he would curl up in our laps and allow himself to be stroked when he was in the mood. Elizabeth loved him and called him "my sweet Ariel," even when he was misbehaving. After she died, he comforted me and affirmed my connection to her for many years. When I was away from home, the family next door would take care of him, and when I came back, there he would be, sitting regally on the brick wall. I liked to think that he was waiting for me, but I knew that he was probably just surveying his domain.

I tell his story in connection to my dream because the dream kittens could have been images of his progeny or his missing brothers and sisters. They were tiny versions of him, incarnations of his fiercely proud and independent spirit. Since they were just starting out in life, they embodied pure feline potential. In the dream they were all alike, but as they developed, they would take on individual characteristics, just as he did as he grew up and his ears and tail turned pale orange. The important thing was to nurture these kittens so that their individuality could emerge and flourish, as his had. In other words, it was up to me to help these imaginal kittens "individuate." But there were so many of them! Nature is prolific and provided an abundant supply of infant felines for me to nurture. Some would thrive, but some, like Elizabeth, might not survive into full adulthood. Nevertheless, many would grow up to display their unique markings, temperamental quirks, and behavioral habits. In the paradoxical process of individuation, each would become a unique representative of its species, yet retain the unmistakable essence of "catness."

Cats in dreams, myths, and fairy tales are often interpreted as images of feminine elegance and grace. In ancient Egypt, for example, the goddess Bastet, protectress of home, mothers, and children, was depicted in cat form.[2] Ariel, however, was most definitely a male cat. He was elegant and graceful, but there was nothing feminine about him. He was the epitome of masculine energy, focus, and drive. By pointing to the white kittens, Elizabeth may have been hinting that my young masculine energy was in "pretty good shape," but still needed nurturance and protection. Like the kittens, it was still in its infancy. There was potential there, but the attainment of full power was a work in progress.

The next section of the dream has to do with the new name and title that Elizabeth has earned. In myths and biblical stories, characters are given a new name to signify an inner transformation following hardships endured and accomplishments achieved. For example, in John 1:42 Simon's name is changed to Peter when he becomes Jesus's disciple. Saul becomes Paul after his conversion to Christianity (Acts 13:9), and Jacob acquires the name "Israel" after he wrestles with the angel (Gen. 32:24–29).[3] Elizabeth's new name and title suggest that she has accomplished her "challenging and satisfying work" and has achieved a new status. She is quite shy when she tells me about this, but it is clear that she is happy and proud of what she has done. I cannot pronounce her words, but I comprehend the meaning of what she is saying. Like Jung's last dream of his father, this dream suggests that dream images of the dead speak a language that the living cannot understand. The reference to language is also present in von Franz's dream of her dead father (see Chapter 5), in which her father responds to her question about his happiness by saying, "Let me remember what you, the living, call happy. Yes, in your language, I am happy."[4] The implication is that the language of mere mortals is inadequate to describe the experience of the dead. A new language is required, one that we will not learn until we join them in "the place where they are now."

In the biblical accounts cited above, the bestowing of new names indicates the acquisition of a new identity. But the achievement of a new identity also involves separation from and loss of the old one. When a loved one dies, our identity in relationship to that person changes radically. I will always be Elizabeth's mother, but my sense of myself as the mother of a living child and the mother of a child who has died are very different. In connection with this change in identity I think of a quote from a "noble Abyssinian woman," cited by Kerenyi:

> She is and remains a mother even though her child die, though all her children die. For at one time she carried the child under her heart. And it does not go out of her heart ever again. Not even when it is dead.[5]

Bereaved mothers belong to a vast but invisible community of women linked by a common experience that we did not wish to have. We will always be mothers and will carry the images of our children in our hearts, just as we once carried their bodies in our wombs. But when one experiences the death of a child, one's maternal self-image "dies" as well, and a new one gradually takes its place. Some, like Charlotte Mathes, identify with the image of the Pietà or the figure of the Mater Dolorosa, the Mother of Sorrows. I found solace in the figure of the goddess Demeter, who would not cease grieving until she had regained her lost daughter. Paradoxically, my connection with that ancient myth helped me transfer my attachment from Elizabeth's living being to the images of her that appeared in my dreams. It was as though she became the "Kore" for me—not a literal daughter, but an archetypal image of the Eternal Maiden who lives in my psyche now. In my final dream of her, she transfers my mothering role from herself to the kittens. She has a new identity now, and so do I. In this context, both the kittens and my new role can be seen as two more parting gifts from her. After this dream, the imaginal kittens became my "children" and provided me with new creative energy and a new sense of purpose.

After she tells me about her new name and title, Elizabeth asks for my blessing. She seems to be concerned that her father and I will be upset or angry that she is no longer using the name we had given her. But in fact, I am not upset at all. She will always be "Elizabeth" to me, but I am honored to affirm her new identity and title. The word "blessing," derived from the Old English *blēdsian and* based on *blōd* 'blood,' may originally have meant "to mark or consecrate with blood."[6] In connection with this definition, I am reminded of the three drops of blood on the sand in my premonitory dream (see Chapter 2). Perhaps that blood can now be used to consecrate her transformation. I bless her with a touch of humor, blowing on my fingers and rubbing them on my shirt in the age-old gesture that means, "Good for you!" But as soon as I do this, the bubble bursts and she is gone. Then, as in other dreams, I begin to laugh and cry at once, but this time my tears are tears of joy. When a group of women approaches, I exclaim, "She was here! It wasn't a dream, it was a vision!" Then I wake up, eager to tell people about what has happened.

After this dream, I knew that the time had come for me to begin to speak and write about my grief dreams. Enough time had elapsed since Elizabeth's death that I could do it with a calm voice and dry eyes, although I confess there were moments when my voice quavered and my eyes filled up. In my dream of the underworld Elizabeth had said, "Tell people about me!" and I have tried to honor her request by presenting lectures and workshops, writing my first book, and now writing this revised edition. Doing this work has convinced me that we, the living, can encounter the dead in the realm of images, a dimension of reality that exists beyond the bounds of space, time, and waking consciousness. There we can embrace again, share our grief, come to terms with death, give and receive messages and gifts, and say our final goodbyes. The process takes a very long time, and I am not sure that it will ever be over. Perhaps one day, when my own death comes, I will meet Elizabeth again in the land of shades. Perhaps, like her, I will learn to understand and speak a new language. Until that day comes, I will treasure my dreams and be grateful for all they have taught me about life, death, and enduring love.

Notes

1   W. Shakespeare, *The Tempest*, 1.2.206.
2   *The Herder Symbol Dictionary*, trans. B.Matthews, 32–33.
3   *The Holy Bible*, King James version.
4   C. G. Jung and C. Kerényi, *Essays on a Science of Mythology*, 101.
5   M.-L. von Franz, *On Dreams and Death*, 112.
6   *New Oxford American Dictionary*, computer application.

Bibliography

Theodor Abt and Erik Hornung, *Knowledge for the Afterlife: The Egyptian* Amduat—*a Quest for Immortality*. Zürich: Living Human Heritage Publications, 2003.

Emily M. Ahern, *The Cult of the Dead in a Chinese Village*. Stanford, CA: Stanford University Press, 1973.

Dante Alighieri, *The Divine Comedy*, trans. John Ciardi. New York: American Library, 2003.

Deirdre Bair, *Jung: A Biography*. Boston, MA: Little, Brown and Company, 2003.

John Bowlby, "Grief and Mourning in Infancy and Early Childhood," in *The Psychoanalytic Study of the Child 15* (1960).

Joseph Campbell, *The Hero with a Thousand Faces*. Princeton, NJ: Princeton University Press, 1949.

Pam Cope with Aimee Molloy, *Jantsen's Gift: A True Story of Grief, Rescue, and Grace*. New York: Hachette Book Group, 2009.

Henri Corbin, "*Mundus Imaginalis*, or The Imaginary and the Imaginal," in *Swedenborg and Esoteric Islam*, trans. Leonard Fox. West Chester, PA: The Swedenborg Foundation, 1995.

Alan Cowell, "A Suicide Bomb, a Dead Daughter and a Test of Faith," in *The New York Times*, May 6, 2006.

Loring M. Danforth and Alexander Tsiaras, *The Death Rituals of Rural Greece*. Princeton, NJ: Princeton University Press, 1982.

A. De Vries, *Dictionary of Symbols and Imagery*. Amsterdam and London: North Holland Publishing Co., 1974.

Joan Didion, *Blue Nights*. New York: Alfred A. Knopf, 2011.

Joan Didion, *The Year of Magical Thinking*. New York: Alfred A. Knopf, 2005.

Edward F. Edinger, *Anatomy of the Psyche: Alchemical Symbolism in Psychotherapy*. La Salle, IL: Open Court, 1985.

Sigmund Freud, "Formulations Regarding the Two Principles in Mental Functioning," in *Collected Papers*, IV. London: Hogarth Press, 1950.

Sigmund Freud, *The Interpretation of Dreams*, ed. and trans. James Strachey. New York: Avon Books, 1965.

Sigmund Freud, "Mourning and Melancholia," in *The Penguin Freud Reader*, ed. Adam Phillips. London: Penguin Books, 2006.

Marija Gimbutas, *The Language of the Goddess*. San Francisco, CA: Harper and Row, 1989.

Elaine Gonzalez, "In Search of Chocolate: Mexico's Sacred Legacy," www.elainegonzalez.com, 1994.

Robert Graves, *The Greek Myths*, Vol. 1. Baltimore, MD: Penguin Books, 1955.

The Brothers Grimm, *The Complete Fairy Tales of the Brothers Grimm,* trans. Jack Zipes. New York: Bantam Books, 1987.

Stanislav Grof, *Books of the Dead: Manuals for Living and Dying.* London: Thames & Hudson, 1994.

Geri Grubbs, *Bereavement Dreaming and the Individuating Soul.* Berwick, ME: Nicholas-Hays, Inc., 2004.

Barbara Hannah, *The Cat, Dog, and Horse Lectures,* ed. Dean L. Frantz. Wilmette, IL: Chiron Publications, 1992.

M. Esther Harding, *Woman's Mysteries: Ancient and Modern.* New York: Harper & Row, 1971.

Robert Hellenga, *The Fall of a Sparrow.* New York: Scribner Paperback Fiction, Simon & Schuster, 1998.

The Herder Symbol Dictionary, trans. Boris Matthews. Wilmette, IL: Chiron Publications, 1986.

The Holy Bible, King James Version. Nashville, Dallas, Mexico City, Rio de Janeiro: Thomas Nelson, Inc., 1982, 2007, 2010.

Homer, "Hymn to Demeter," in *Homeric Hymns,* trans. Michael Crudden. Oxford, UK: Oxford University Press, 2001.

Homer, *The Iliad of Homer,* trans. Robert Fitzgerald. Garden City, NY: Anchor Press/ Doubleday, 1975.

Homer, *The Odyssey,* trans. Robert Fitzgerald. Garden City, NY: Anchor Books, Doubleday & Company, Inc., 1963.

The I Ching, or Book of Changes, trans. Richard Wilhelm, English trans. Cary F. Baynes. Princeton, NJ: Princeton University Press, 1977.

Aniela Jaffé, *Apparitions: An Archetypal Approach to Death Dreams and Ghosts.* Irving, TX: Spring Publications, 1979.

Gertrude Jobes, *Dictionary of Mythology, Folklore, and Symbols.* New York: The Scarecrow Press, 1962.

C. G. Jung, *Aion,* CW 9ii, 2nd edition, trans. R. F. C. Hull. London: Routledge and Kegan Paul, 1968.

C. G. Jung, *The Archetypes and the Collective Unconscious,* CW 9i, 2nd edition, trans. R. F. C. Hull. London: Routledge and Kegan Paul, 1968.

C. G. Jung, *C. G. Jung Speaking: Interviews and Encounters,* eds. William McGuire and R. F. C. Hull. Princeton, N. J.: Princeton University Press, Bollingen Series XCVII, 1977.

C. G. Jung, *Memories, Dreams, Reflections,* ed. Aniela Jaffé, trans. Richard and Clara Winston. London: Fontana Paperbacks, Flamingo edition, Random House, 1983.

C. G. Jung, "On the Psychology and Pathology of Occult Phenomena," *Psychiatric Studies,* 2nd edition. *The Collected Works of C. G. Jung,* Vol. 1, trans. R. F. C. Hull. London and Henley: Routledge and Kegan Paul, 1970.

C. G. Jung, "Psychological Commentary," in *The Tibetan Book of the Dead,* ed. W. Y. Evans-Wentz. London: Oxford University Press, 1960.

C. G. Jung, *The Red Book (Liber Novus),* ed. Sonu Shamdasani. New York and London: W. W. Norton & Company, 2009.

C. G. Jung, *The Symbolic Life,* CW 18, trans. R.F. C. Hull. London: Routledge and Kegan Paul, 1977.

C. G. Jung, *Symbols of Transformation,* CW 5, 2nd edition, trans. R. F. C. Hull. London and Henley: Routledge and Kegan Paul, 1981.

C. G. Jung, *Two Essays on Analytical Psychology*, CW 7, 2nd edition, trans. R. F. C. Hull. London and Henley: Routledge and Kegan Paul, 1966.

C. G. Jung and C. Kerényi, *Essays on a Science of Mythology*, Bollingen Series XXII, trans. R. F. C. Hull. Princeton, NJ: Princeton University Press, 1969 [1963].

Donald Kalsched, *The Inner World of Trauma: Archetypal Defenses of the Personal Spirit*. London and New York: Routledge, 1996.

Verena Kast, *A Time to Mourn: Growing through the Grief Process*. Einsiedeln, Switzerland: Daimon Verlag, 1988.

John Keats, letter to his brothers George and Thomas Keats, December, 1817, in *John Keats: Selected Poems and Letters*, ed. Douglas Bush. Boston, MA: Houghton Mifflin Company, 1959.

Emmanuel X. Kennedy, "The Alchemy of Death," unpublished diploma thesis presented to the C. G. Jung Institute, Zürich, 1988.

Melanie Klein, "Mourning and its Relation to Manic-Depressive States," in *International Journal of Psychoanalysis 21* (1940).

Elisabeth Kubler-Ross, *On Death and Dying*. New York: Macmillan, 1969.

Paul Kugler, *Raids on the Unthinkable: Freudian and Jungian Psychoanalyses*. New Orleans, LA: Spring Journal Books, 2005.

Peter A. Levine, *Waking the Tiger: Healing Trauma*. Berkeley, CA: North Atlantic Books, 1997.

Margaret Mahler, *The Psychological Birth of the Human Infant*. New York: Basic Books, 1975.

Karyn Maier, *The Symbolic Meaning of the Ginkgo Tree*, <www.gardenguides.com>, March 18, 2018.

Marilyn Marshall, "A 'Close-Up' of the Kiss," in *Spring 73, Cinema and Psyche*. New Orleans, LA: Spring Journal, 2005.

Charlotte Mathes, *And a Sword Shall Pierce Your Heart: Moving from Despair to Meaning after the Death of a Child*. Wilmette, IL: Chiron Publications, 2006.

Anne McCracken and Mary Semel, eds., *A Broken Heart Still Beats: After Your Child Dies*. Center City, MN: Hazelden, 1998.

Greg Mogenson, "The Afterlife of the Image," in *Spring 71, Orpheus*. New Orleans, LA: Spring Journal, 2004.

Greg Mogenson, *Greeting the Angels: An Imaginal View of the Mourning Process*. Amityville, NY: Baywood Publishing Co., 1992.

Erich Neumann, *The Great Mother*. Princeton, NJ: Princeton University Press, 1955.

Julie Nicholson, *A Song for Jenny*. New York: HarperCollins, 2011.

Colin M. Parkes, *Bereavement: Studies of Grief in Adult Life*, 3rd edition. Philadelphia, PA: Taylor & Francis, 2001 [1996].

Sylvia Brinton Perera, *Descent to the Goddess*. Toronto: Inner City Books, 1981.

Rainer Maria Rilke, *Duino Elegies*, trans. David Young. New York and London: W. W. Norton & Company, 1978.

Rainer Maria Rilke, *Letters to a Young Poet*, trans. Reginald Snell. Mineola, NY: Dover Publications, 2002.

Judith Savage, *Mourning Unlived Lives: A Psychological Study of Childbearing Loss*. Wilmette, IL: Chiron Publications, 1989.

William Shakespeare, *The Complete Poems and Plays of William Shakespeare*, ed. William Allan Nielson and Charles Jarvis Hill. Cambridge, MA: The Riverside Press, 1942.

Murray Stein, *In Midlife: A Jungian Perspective*. Dallas, TX: Spring Publications, 1983.

Paul Tillich, *Systematic Theology*, Vol. I. Chicago, IL: The University of Chicago Press, 1951.

J. R. R. Tolkien, *The Letters of J. R. R. Tolkien*, ed. Humphrey Carpenter. Boston, MA: Houghton Mifflin Company, 1981.

J. R. R. Tolkien, *The Return of the King*. Boston and New York: Houghton Mifflin Company, 1994 [1955].

Bessel A. van der Kolk, Alexander C. McFarlane, and Lars Weisaeth, eds., *Traumatic Stress*. New York: The Guilford Press, 1996.

Marie-Louise von Franz, *On Dreams and Death*, trans. Emmanuel X. Kennedy and Vernon Brooks. Boston, MA: Shambhala Publications, 1988.

Barbara Walker, *The Woman's Dictionary of Symbols and Sacred Objects*. New York: HarperSanFrancisco, 1988.

D. W. Winnicott, *Playing and Reality*. London: Tavistock Publications, 1971.

William Wordsworth, *The Poetical Works of Wordsworth*, ed. Thomas Hutchinson. London: Oxford University Press, 1960.

Jerry R. Wright, "Archetypal *Thin Places*: Experiencing the Numinosum." Thesis submitted to the Inter-Regional Society of Jungian Analysts, 2000.

William Butler Yeats, *The Collected Poems of W. B. Yeats*. New York: Macmillan, 1958.

Index

For Product Safety Concerns and Information please contact our EU
representative GPSR@taylorandfrancis.com
Taylor & Francis Verlag GmbH, Kaufingerstraße 24, 80331 München, Germany

www.ingramcontent.com/pod-product-compliance
Lightning Source LLC
Chambersburg PA
CBHW050523280326
41932CB00014B/2425